Quick & Easy
Barbecue

p

Contents

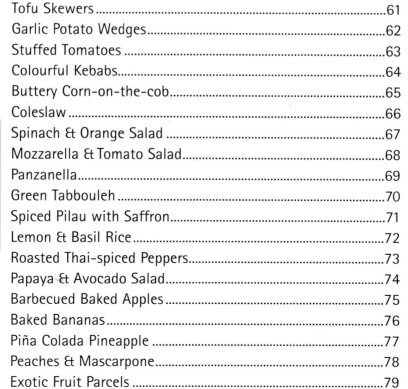

Introduction

What is it that makes a meal cooked outdoors over burning coals so appetizing? Perhaps it is the fresh air or the tantalizing aroma or the sound of food sizzling on the cooking rack. Whatever it is, there is no doubt that barbecues and outdoor grills are becoming more and more popular. This is hardly surprising when you see just how many wonderful dishes can be cooked over charcoal. This book alone contains 120 recipes, leaving you with no shortage of inspiration.

Gone are the days when sausages and burgers were the staple of every barbecue party, although traditionalists will find recipes here for making fabulous burgers and for tangy sauces to serve with the sausages. But why not try fish, which cooks to perfection on the barbecue or grill and is healthy too? There are also dozens of tasty marinades and bastes for meat lovers, as well as vegetarian dishes, salads and side dishes. You can even cook a dessert on the barbecue.

Which barbecue or outdoor grill?

You do not need a large, sophisticated barbecue to produce mouthwatering food, although once you have tried some of these recipes you might want to invest in something larger.

Essentially barbecues are an open fire with a rack set over the hot coals, on which the food is cooked. You can improvise a makeshift barbecue with nothing more complicated than a few house bricks and an old oven rack. Chicken wire and baking racks can also be used to cook on. Purpose-made barbecues or outdoor grills are, however, available in all shapes and sizes, from small disposable trays to large wagon models, powered by bottled gas.

As the names suggest, portable and semi-portable barbecues tend to be small. Some types have a stand or folding legs; others have fixed legs. If you have a small model and are cooking for large numbers, cook the food in rotation so that guests can begin on the first course while the second batch is cooking.

Most brazier barbecues, which stand on long legs and have a wind shield, are light and portable. On some models the height of the rack can be varied, and some types incorporate rotisseries.

Covered barbecues or outdoor grills are essential if you want to cook whole joints of meat. The lid completely covers the barbecue, increasing the temperature at which food cooks and acting, in effect, like an oven. The temperature is controlled by air vents. When used without the cover, these barbecues are treated like traditional barbecues.

Wagon barbecues or outdoor grills are larger and more sophisticated. They have wheels and often incorporate a handy tabletop.

Electric or gas barbecues or grills heat volcanic lava coals. The flavour is still good, because the flavour of barbecued food comes from the aromas of fat and

juices burning on the coals rather than just from the fuel itself.

Equipment

Apart from the barbecue itself, you do not need any special equipment, but do arm yourself with a pair of oven gloves. Long-handled tools can be useful, as well as being safer and more convenient to use. They are not expensive, and if you cook on a barbecue regularly it is a good idea to invest in a set. Specially shaped racks for burgers, sausages and fish are useful but not essential.

You will need a set of skewers if you want to cook kebabs. Metal skewers should be flat to stop the food slipping round as it cooks. Remember that metal skewers get very hot, so wear gloves or use tongs to turn them. Wooden skewers are much cheaper than metal skewers but are not always very long lasting. Always soak wooden skewers in cold water for at least 30 minutes before use to help prevent them from burning on the barbecue and then cover the exposed ends with pieces of kitchen foil.
A water spray is useful for cooling down coals or dampening down flare-ups.

Lighting the barbecue

Charcoal is the most popular fuel although you can use wood. Charcoal is available as lump wood, which is irregular in shape and size but easy to light, or as briquettes, which burn for longer and with a more uniform heat but are harder to light.

Light the barbecue at least an hour before you want to start cooking. Stack the coals in the pan and use specially designed solid or liquid lighter fuels to help set the charcoal alight. Do not use household fire lighters because these will taint the food. Never use paraffin or petrol to light a barbecue – it is very dangerous if used incorrectly.

The barbecue is ready to use when the flames have died down and the burning coals are covered with a white ash.

When the coals are ready, spread them out into a uniform layer, so that the barbecue gives an even heat.

Preparing to cook

Before you begin to cook, oil the rack so that the food does not stick to it. Do this away from the barbecue or grill or the oil will flare up as it drips on to the coals. For most dishes, position the rack about 7.5 cm/3 inches above the coals. Raise the rack if you want to slow down the cooking. If you cannot adjust the height of the rack, slow down the cooking by spreading out the coals or moving the food to the edges of the rack.

If your barbecue has air vents, use them to control the temperature – open the vents for more heat, close them to reduce the temperature.

It is very difficult to give exact times for cooking on a barbecue, so use the times given in the recipes in this book as a guide only. Always test the food to make sure that it is cooked thoroughly before serving.

KEY

 Simplicity level 1–3 (1 easiest, 3 slightly harder)

 Preparation time

 Cooking time

Lemon Monkfish Skewers

A simple basting sauce is brushed over these tasty kebabs. When served with crusty bread, they make a perfect light meal.

NUTRITIONAL INFORMATION

Calories 191	Sugars 2g
Protein 21g	Fat 11g
Carbohydrate 1g	Saturates 1g

 10 mins   15 mins

SERVES 4

INGREDIENTS

450 g/1 lb monkfish tail

2 courgettes

1 lemon

12 cherry tomatoes

8 bay leaves

SAUCE

3 tbsp olive oil

2 tbsp lemon juice

1 tsp chopped fresh thyme

½ tsp lemon pepper

salt

TO SERVE

green salad leaves

fresh, crusty bread

1 Cut the monkfish tail into 5 cm/ 2 inch chunks.

2 Cut the courgettes into thick slices and the lemon into wedges.

3 Thread the monkfish, courgettes, lemon, tomatoes and bay leaves on to 4 skewers.

4 To make the basting sauce, combine the oil, lemon juice, thyme, lemon pepper and salt to taste in a small bowl.

5 Brush the basting sauce liberally all over the skewers.

6 Cook the skewers on the barbecue for about 15 minutes over medium-hot coals, basting them frequently with the sauce, until the fish is cooked through. Transfer the skewers to plates and serve with plenty of green salad leaves and wedges of crusty bread.

VARIATION

Use plaice fillets instead of the monkfish, if you prefer. Allow two fillets per person, and skin and cut each fillet lengthways into two. Roll up each piece and thread them on to the skewers.

Smoky Fish Skewers

The combination of fresh and smoked fish gives these kebabs a special flavour. Choose thick fish fillets for good, bite-sized chunks.

NUTRITIONAL INFORMATION

Calories 221	Sugars 0g
Protein 33g	Fat 10g
Carbohydrate 0g	Saturates 1g

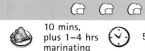

10 mins, plus 1–4 hrs marinating   5–10 mins

SERVES 4

INGREDIENTS

350 g/12 oz smoked cod fillet

350 g/12 oz cod fillet

8 large raw prawns

8 bay leaves

fresh dill, to garnish (optional)

MARINADE

4 tbsp sunflower oil, plus a little for brushing

2 tbsp lemon or lime juice

grated rind of ½ lemon or lime

¼ tsp dried dill

salt and pepper

1 Skin both types of cod and cut the flesh into bite-sized pieces. Peel the prawns, leaving just the tail.

2 To make the marinade, combine the oil, lemon or lime juice and rind, dill and salt and pepper to taste in a shallow, non-metallic dish.

3 Place the prepared fish in the marinade and stir together until the fish is well coated on all sides. Leave the fish to marinate for 1–4 hours.

4 Thread the fish on to 4 skewers, alternating the 2 types of cod with the prawns and bay leaves.

5 Cover the barbecue rack with lightly oiled kitchen foil and place the fish skewers on top of the foil.

6 Barbecue the fish skewers over hot coals for 5–10 minutes, basting with any remaining marinade, turning once.

7 Garnish the skewers with fresh dill (if using) and serve immediately.

COOK'S TIP

Cod fillet can be rather flaky, so choose the thicker end which is easier to cut into chunky pieces. Cook the fish on kitchen foil rather than directly on the rack, so that if the fish breaks away from the skewer, it is not wasted.

Mediterranean Sardines

These tasty sardines will bring back memories of Mediterranean holidays. Serve them with crusty brown bread as a perfect starter.

NUTRITIONAL INFORMATION

Calories	857	Sugars	.........0g
Protein	........88g	Fat	..........56g
Carbohydrate	....0g	Saturates	......11g

 15 mins, plus 30 mins marinating 6–8 mins

SERVES 4

I N G R E D I E N T S

8–12 fresh sardines

8–12 sprigs of fresh thyme

3 tbsp lemon juice

4 tbsp olive oil

salt and pepper

T O G A R N I S H

lemon wedges

tomato slices

fresh herbs

1 Clean and gut the fish if this has not already been done by the fishmonger.

2 Remove the scales from the sardines by rubbing the back of a knife from tail to head along the body. Wash the sardines and pat dry with absorbent kitchen paper.

3 Tuck a sprig of fresh thyme into the body of each sardine.

4 Transfer the sardines to a large, non-metallic dish and season with salt and pepper to taste.

5 Beat together the lemon juice and oil in a bowl and pour the mixture over the sardines. Leave in the refrigerator to marinate for about 30 minutes.

6 Remove the sardines from the marinade and place them in a hinged basket, if you have one, or on a rack. Barbecue the sardines over hot coals for 3–4 minutes on each side, basting frequently with any remaining marinade.

7 Serve the cooked sardines garnished with lemon wedges, tomato slices and fresh herbs.

VARIATION

For a slightly different flavour and texture, give the sardines a crispy coating by tossing them in dried breadcrumbs and basting them with a little olive oil.

Lemon Herrings

Cooking these fish in foil parcels gives them a wonderfully moist texture. They make a perfect dinner party starter.

NUTRITIONAL INFORMATION

Calories 355   Sugars 0g
Protein . . . . .19g   Fat 31g
Carbohydrate . . . .0g   Saturates 13g

 5 mins   15–20 mins

SERVES 4

I N G R E D I E N T S

4 herrings, gutted and scaled

4 bay leaves

salt

1 lemon, sliced

4 tbsp unsalted butter

2 tbsp chopped fresh parsley

½ tsp lemon pepper

fresh crusty bread, to serve

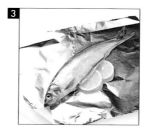

1 Season the prepared herrings inside and out with freshly ground salt to taste. (To scale the fish, see Step 2, page 8.)

2 Place a bay leaf inside the cavity of each fish.

3 Place 4 squares of foil on the work surface and divide the lemon slices evenly among them. Place a fish on top of the lemon slices on each of the foil squares.

4 Beat the butter until softened, then mix in the parsley and lemon pepper. Dot the flavoured butter liberally all over the fish.

5 Wrap the fish tightly in the kitchen foil and barbecue over medium-hot coals for 15–20 minutes or until the fish is

cooked through – the flesh should be white in colour and firm to the touch (unwrap the foil to check, then re-wrap).

6 Transfer the wrapped fish parcels to individual, warm serving plates.

7 Unwrap the foil parcels just before serving and serve the fish with fresh, crusty bread to mop up the deliciously flavoured cooking juices.

VARIATION

For a main course use trout instead of herring. Cook the trout for 20–30 minutes until the flesh is opaque and firm to the touch.

Stuffed Mushrooms

Large mushrooms have more flavour than the smaller button mushrooms. Serve these mushrooms as a side vegetable or starter.

NUTRITIONAL INFORMATION

Calories	148	Sugars	.........1g
Protein	........11g	Fat	...........7g
Carbohydrate	....11g	Saturates	......3g

10 mins   10 mins

SERVES 4

INGREDIENTS

12 open-cap mushrooms

4 spring onions, chopped

4 tsp olive oil

100 g/3½ oz fresh brown breadcrumbs

1 tsp chopped fresh oregano

100 g/3½ oz low-fat mature
  Cheddar cheese

1 Wash the mushrooms and pat dry with kitchen paper. Remove the stalks and chop the stalks finely.

2 Sauté the mushroom stalks and chopped spring onions in half of the oil. Transfer to a large mixing bowl.

3 Add the breadcrumbs and oregano to the mushrooms and spring onions, mix and set aside.

4 Crumble the cheese into small pieces in a small bowl. Add the cheese to the breadcrumb mixture and mix well. Spoon the stuffing mixture into the mushroom caps.

5 Drizzle the remaining oil over the mushrooms. Barbecue on an oiled rack over medium-hot coals for 10 minutes or until cooked through.

6 Transfer the mushrooms to serving plates and serve immediately while hot.

VARIATION

For a change replace the cheese with finely-chopped chorizo sausage (remove the skin first), chopped hard-boiled eggs, chopped olives or chopped anchovy fillets. Mop up the juices with some crusty bread.

Prawn Skewers with Salsa

Prawns of all sizes are popular fare in the Mediterranean, where they are often cooked very simply by grilling – the key is not to overcook them.

NUTRITIONAL INFORMATION

Calories	135	Sugars	........4g
Protein	.........6g	Fat	...........11g
Carbohydrate	....4g	Saturates	.......2g

10 mins, plus 15 mins chilling   2–2½ mins

MAKES 8

INGREDIENTS

32 large tiger prawns

olive oil, for brushing

aïoli to serve (see page 12)

MARINADE

125 ml/4 fl oz extra virgin olive oil

2 tbsp lemon juice

1 tsp finely chopped red chilli

1 tsp balsamic vinegar

pepper

TOMATO SALSA

2 large sun-ripened tomatoes, skinned, cored, deseeded and chopped

4 spring onions, white parts only, very finely chopped

1 red pepper, skinned, deseeded and chopped

1 orange or yellow pepper, skinned, deseeded and chopped

1 tbsp extra virgin olive oil

2 tsp balsamic vinegar

4 sprigs fresh basil

1 To make the marinade, place all the ingredients in a non-metallic bowl and whisk together. Set aside.

2 To prepare the prawns, break off the heads. Peel off the shells, leaving the tails intact. Using a small knife, make a slit along the back and remove the thin black vein. Add the prawns to the marinade and stir until well coated. Cover and chill for 15 minutes.

3 Make the salsa. Put all the ingredients, except the basil, in a non-metallic bowl, toss together and season.

4 Thread 4 prawns on to each of 8 metal skewers, bending each prawn in half. Brush with marinade.

5 Brush a grill rack with oil. Place the skewers on the rack and cook over hot coals, about 7.5 cm/3 inches from the heat source, for 1 minute. Turn the skewers over, brush with marinade again and continue cooking for 1–1½ minutes until the prawns turn pink and opaque.

6 Tear the basil leaves and toss with the salsa. Arrange each skewer on a plate with some salsa and garnish with parsley. Serve with aïoli dip.

Aïoli

This garlic mayonnaise features in many traditional Provençal recipes, but also makes a delicious dip, surrounded by a selection of vegetables.

NUTRITIONAL INFORMATION

Calories	239	Sugars	.......0.1g
Protein	.........1g	Fat	..........26g
Carbohydrate	....1g	Saturates	.......4g

5–6 mins   0 mins

SERVES 4

INGREDIENTS

4 large garlic cloves, or to taste

pinch of sea salt

2 large egg yolks

300 ml/10 fl oz extra virgin olive oil

1–2 tbsp lemon juice, to taste

1 tbsp fresh white breadcrumbs

freshly ground black pepper

TO SERVE (OPTIONAL)

a selection of raw vegetables, such as sliced red peppers, sliced courgettes, whole spring onions and tomato wedges

a selection of blanched and cooled vegetables, such as baby artichoke hearts, cauliflower or broccoli florets or French beans

COOK'S TIP

The amount of garlic in a traditional Provençal aïoli is a matter of personal taste. Local cooks use 2 cloves per person as a rule of thumb, but this version is slightly milder, although still bursting with flavour.

1 Finely chop the garlic, add the salt and use the tip and broad side of a knife to work them into a smooth paste.

2 Transfer the paste to a food processor. Add the egg yolks and blend.

3 With the motor running, slowly pour in the olive oil in a steady stream through the feed tube, processing until a thick mayonnaise forms.

4 Add 1 tablespoon of the lemon juice and the fresh breadcrumbs and process again. Taste and add more lemon juice if necessary. Season to taste.

5 Place the aïoli in a bowl, cover and chill until ready to serve. This will keep for up to 7 days in the refrigerator. To serve as a dip, place the bowl of aïoli on a large platter and surround with a selection of crudités.

Black Bean Nachos

Packed with authentic Mexican flavours, this tasty black bean and cheese dip is fun to eat and will get any meal off to a good start.

NUTRITIONAL INFORMATION

Calories 429   Sugars 2g
Protein ....28g   Fat 24g
Carbohydrate ...25g   Saturates 15g

  5 mins   1 hr 55 mins

SERVES 4

INGREDIENTS

225 g/8 oz dried black beans, soaked overnight and drained, or canned black beans, drained

175–225 g/6–8 oz grated cheese, such as Cheddar, Fontina, pecorino, asiago, or a combination

about ¼ tsp cumin seeds or ground cumin

about 4 tbsp soured cream

thinly sliced pickled jalapeños (optional)

1 tbsp chopped fresh coriander

handful of shredded lettuce

tortilla chips, to serve

1 Put the black beans in a pan, cover with water and bring to the boil. Boil for 10 minutes, then reduce the heat and simmer for about 1½ hours until tender. Drain thoroughly.

2 Spread the cooked black beans in a shallow ovenproof dish, then scatter the cheese over the top. Sprinkle with cumin, to taste.

3 Bake in a preheated oven, 190°C/375°F/Gas Mark 5, for 10–15 minutes, or until the beans are cooked through and the cheese is bubbly and melted.

4 Remove the beans and cheese from the oven and spoon the soured cream on top. Add the jalapeños, if using, and sprinkle with fresh coriander and lettuce.

5 Arrange the tortilla chips around the beans, sticking them into the mixture. Serve the nachos at once.

VARIATION

To add a meaty flavour, spoon chopped and browned chorizo on top of the beans before sprinkling over the cheese, and cook as in step 3. Finely chopped leftover cooked meat can also be added in this way.

Prawn Satay

It is worth seeking a supplier of Thai ingredients, such as lime leaves, as they add distinctive flavours for which there are no real substitutes.

NUTRITIONAL INFORMATION

Calories 367   Sugars 25g
Protein . . . . .9g   Fat 23g
Carbohydrate . . .33g   Saturates 3g

5 mins, plus 8 hrs marinating

7–10 mins

SERVES 4

INGREDIENTS

12 peeled raw king prawns

MARINADE

1 tsp ground coriander

1 tsp ground cumin

2 tbsp light soy sauce

4 tbsp vegetable oil

1 tbsp curry powder

1 tbsp ground turmeric

125 ml/4 fl oz coconut milk

3 tbsp sugar

PEANUT SAUCE

2 tbsp vegetable oil

3 garlic cloves, crushed

1 tbsp Thai red curry paste

125 ml/4 fl oz coconut milk

225 ml/8 fl oz fish or chicken stock

1 tbsp sugar

1 tsp salt

1 tbsp lemon juice

4 tbsp finely chopped unsalted roasted peanuts

4 tbsp dried breadcrumbs

flaked almonds to garnish

1 Slit the prawns down their backs and remove any black veins. Set aside. Mix together the marinade ingredients and add the prawns. Mix well, cover and set aside for at least 8 hours or overnight.

2 To make the peanut sauce, heat the oil in a large frying pan until very hot. Add the garlic and fry until just starting to colour. Add the curry paste and mix well, cooking for a further 30 seconds. Add the coconut milk, stock, sugar, salt and lemon juice and stir well. Boil for 1–2 minutes, stirring constantly. Add the peanuts and breadcrumbs and mix together well. Transfer to a bowl and top with almonds

3 Using 4 skewers, thread 3 prawns on to each. Cook under a preheated hot grill or on the barbecue for 3–4 minutes on each side until just cooked through. Serve immediately with the peanut sauce.

Sticky Ginger Chicken Wings

A finger-licking starter that's ideal for parties – but have some finger bowls ready. If you can't get chicken wings, use drumsticks instead.

NUTRITIONAL INFORMATION

Calories . . . . .416 Sugars 5g
Protein . . . . .41g Fat 25g
Carbohydrate . . . .7g Saturates 7g

5 mins, plus 8 hrs marinating

12–15 mins

SERVES 4

I N G R E D I E N T S

2 garlic cloves, peeled

1 piece stem ginger in syrup

1 tsp coriander seeds

2 tbsp stem ginger syrup

2 tbsp dark soy sauce

1 tbsp lime juice

1 tsp sesame oil

12 chicken wings

lime wedges and fresh coriander leaves, to garnish

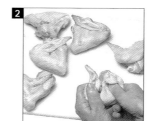

1 Roughly chop the garlic and ginger. In a pestle and mortar, crush the garlic, stem ginger and coriander seeds to a paste, gradually working in the ginger syrup, soy sauce, lime juice and sesame oil.

2 Tuck the pointed tip of each chicken wing underneath the thicker end of the wing to make a neat triangular shape. Place in a large bowl.

3 Add the garlic and ginger paste to the bowl and toss the chicken wings in the mixture to coat evenly. Cover and leave in the refrigerator to marinate for 8 hours or overnight.

4 Arrange the chicken wings in one layer on a foil-covered barbecue rack or grill pan, and barbecue over hot coals or grill under a medium-hot grill for 12–15 minutes, turning occasionally, until golden and cooked through.

5 To serve, garnish with lime wedges and fresh coriander.

Barbecued Chicken Wings

These chicken wings are brushed with a simple barbecue glaze, which can be made in minutes, but will be enjoyed by all.

NUTRITIONAL INFORMATION

Calories	143	Sugars	.........6g
Protein	........14g	Fat	...........7g
Carbohydrate	....6g	Saturates	......1g

🍲 5 mins   🕐 20 mins

SERVES 4

INGREDIENTS

8 chicken wings or 1 chicken cut into 8 portions

3 tbsp tomato purée

3 tbsp brown fruity sauce

1 tbsp white wine vinegar

1 tbsp clear honey

1 tbsp olive oil

1 clove garlic, crushed (optional)

salad leaves, to serve

1 Remove the skin from the chicken wings if you want to reduce the amount of fat in the dish.

2 To make the barbecue glaze, place the tomato purée, brown fruity sauce, white wine vinegar, honey, oil and garlic in a small bowl. Stir all of the ingredients together until they are blended.

3 Brush the barbecue glaze over the chicken and barbecue over hot coals for 15–20 minutes. Turn the chicken portions over occasionally and baste frequently with the barbecue glaze.

4 If the chicken begins to blacken before it is cooked, raise the rack, or move the chicken to a cooler part of the barbecue to slow down the cooking.

5 Transfer the barbecued chicken to warm serving plates and serve with fresh salad leaves.

COOK'S TIP

When poultry is cooked over a very hot barbecue the heat immediately seals in all of the juices, leaving the meat succulent. For this reason make sure that the coals are hot enough before starting to barbecue.

Indian Charred Chicken

An Indian-influenced dish that is delicious served with naan bread and a cucumber raita.

NUTRITIONAL INFORMATION

Calories 228   Sugars 12g
Protein ....28g   Fat 8g
Carbohydrate ...12g   Saturates 2g

 20 mins   10 mins

SERVES 4

I N G R E D I E N T S

4 chicken breasts, skinned and boned

2 tbsp curry paste

1 tbsp sunflower oil

1 tbsp light muscovado sugar

1 tsp ground ginger

½ tsp ground cumin

TO SERVE

naan bread

green salad leaves

CUCUMBER RAITA

¼ cucumber

salt

150 ml/5 fl oz low-fat natural yogurt

¼ tsp chilli powder

1 Place the chicken breasts between 2 sheets of baking paper or clingfilm. Pound them with the flat side of a meat mallet or rolling pin to flatten them.

2 Mix together the curry paste, oil, sugar, ginger and cumin in a small bowl. Spread the mixture over both sides of the chicken and set aside until required.

3 To make the raita, peel the cucumber and scoop out the seeds with a spoon. Grate the cucumber flesh, sprinkle with salt, place in a sieve and leave to stand for 10 minutes. Rinse off the salt and squeeze out any remaining moisture by pressing the cucumber with the base of a glass or the back of a spoon.

4 In a small bowl, mix the grated cucumber with the natural yogurt and stir in the chilli powder. Leave to chill until required.

5 Transfer the chicken to an oiled rack and barbecue over hot coals for 10 minutes, turning once.

6 Warm the naan bread at the side of the barbecue.

7 Serve the chicken with the naan bread, raita, and fresh salad leaves.

  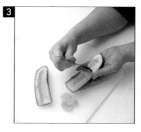

Sweet Maple Chicken

You can use any chicken portions for this recipe. Boned thighs are economical for large barbecues, but wings or drumsticks are also suitable.

NUTRITIONAL INFORMATION

Calories	122	Sugars	........16g
Protein	........11g	Fat	...........1g
Carbohydrate	...17g	Saturates	.......1g

 5 mins   20 mins

SERVES 6

INGREDIENTS

12 boned chicken thighs

5 tbsp maple syrup

1 tbsp caster sugar

grated rind and juice of ½ orange

2 tbsp tomato ketchup

2 tsp Worcestershire sauce

TO GARNISH

slices of orange

sprig of flat leaf parsley

TO SERVE

focaccia bread

salad leaves

cherry tomatoes, quartered

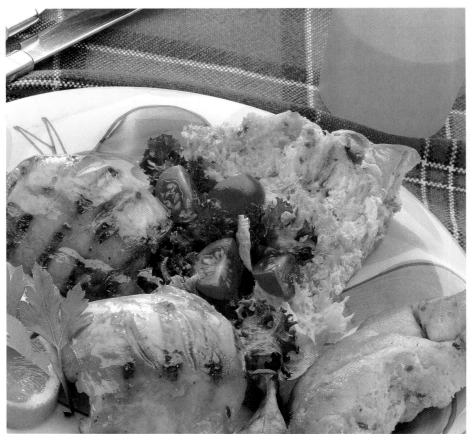

1 Using a sharp knife, make 2–3 slashes in the flesh of the chicken. Place the chicken in a shallow, non-metallic dish.

COOK'S TIP

If time is short you can omit the marinating time. If you use chicken quarters, rather than the smaller thigh portions, parboil them for 10 minutes before brushing with the marinade and barbecueing.

2 To make the marinade, mix together the maple syrup, sugar, orange rind and juice, ketchup and Worcestershire sauce in a small bowl.

3 Pour the marinade over the chicken, tossing the meat to coat thoroughly. Cover and chill until required.

4 Remove the meat from the marinade, reserving the marinade for basting.

5 Place the chicken on the barbecue and cook over hot coals for 20 minutes, turning the meat and basting with the marinade frequently.

6 Transfer the chicken to serving plates and garnish with slices of orange and a sprig of fresh flat leaf parsley. Serve with focaccia bread, fresh salad leaves and cherry tomatoes.

Lemon Chicken Skewers

A tangy lemon yogurt spiced with coriander is served with these tasty marinaded chicken kebabs.

NUTRITIONAL INFORMATION

Calories 187	Sugars 6g
Protein 34g	Fat 3g
Carbohydrate 6g	Saturates 1g

5 mins, plus 2 hrs chilling   15 mins

SERVES 4

I N G R E D I E N T S

4 chicken breasts, skinned and boned

1 tsp ground coriander

2 tsp lemon juice

300 ml/10 fl oz natural yogurt

1 lemon

2 tbsp chopped fresh coriander

oil for brushing

salt and pepper

4 sprigs of fresh coriander, to garnish

TO SERVE

lemon wedges

salad leaves

1 Cut the chicken into 2.5 cm/1 inch pieces and place them in a shallow, non-metallic dish.

2 Add the ground coriander, lemon juice, salt and pepper to taste and 4 tablespoons of the yogurt to the chicken and mix together until thoroughly combined. Cover and leave to chill for at least 2 hours, preferably overnight.

3 To make the lemon yogurt, peel and finely chop the lemon, discarding any pips. Stir the lemon into the yogurt together with the fresh coriander. Leave to chill in the refrigerator until required.

4 Thread the chicken pieces on to skewers. Brush the rack with oil and barbecue the chicken over hot coals for about 15 minutes, basting with the oil.

5 Transfer the chicken kebabs to warm serving plates and garnish with a sprig of fresh coriander, lemon wedges and salad leaves. Serve with the lemon yogurt.

VARIATION
These kebabs are delicious served on a bed of blanched spinach, which has been seasoned with salt, pepper and nutmeg.

Turkey with Cheesy Pockets

Wrapping bacon around the turkey adds extra flavour, and helps to keep the cheese enclosed in the pocket.

NUTRITIONAL INFORMATION

Calories	518	Sugars	.........0g
Protein	........66g	Fat	..........28g
Carbohydrate	....0g	Saturates	.......9g

🍖 10 mins   🕐 20 mins

SERVES 4

INGREDIENTS

4 turkey breast pieces, about 225 g/8 oz each

4 portions full-fat cheese (such as Bel Paese), 15 g/½ oz each

4 sage leaves or ½ tsp dried sage

8 rashers rindless streaky bacon

4 tbsp olive oil

2 tbsp lemon juice

salt and pepper

TO SERVE

garlic bread

salad leaves

cherry tomatoes

1 Carefully cut a pocket into the side of each turkey breast. Open out each breast a little and season inside with salt and pepper to taste.

2 Place a portion of cheese into each pocket. Tuck a sage leaf into each pocket, or sprinkle with a little dried sage.

3 Stretch the bacon out with the back of a knife. Wrap 2 pieces around each turkey breast, covering the pocket.

4 Mix together the oil and lemon juice in a small bowl.

5 Barbecue the turkey over medium-hot coals, 10 minutes each side, basting frequently with the lemon mixture.

6 Place the garlic bread at the side of the barbecue and toast lightly.

7 Transfer the turkey to warm serving plates. Serve with the toasted garlic bread, salad leaves and cherry tomatoes.

VARIATION

You can vary the cheese you use to stuff the turkey – try grated mozzarella or slices of Brie or Camembert. Also try 1 teaspoon of redcurrant jelly or cranberry sauce in each pocket instead of the sage.

Duck with Pineapple Salsa

A salsa is a cross between a sauce and a relish. Salsas are easy to prepare and will liven up all kinds of simple grilled meats.

NUTRITIONAL INFORMATION

Calories 668	Sugars 16g
Protein 41g	Fat 35g
Carbohydrate ...78g	Saturates 15g

5 mins, plus 1 hr marinating   40–45 mins

SERVES 2

I N G R E D I E N T S

2 tbsp Dijon mustard

1 tsp paprika

½ tsp ground ginger

½ tsp ground nutmeg

2 tbsp dark muscovado sugar

2 duckling halves

salad leaves, to serve

S A L S A

225 g/8 oz canned pineapple in natural juice

2 tbsp dark muscovado sugar

1 small red onion, finely chopped

1 red chilli, deseeded and chopped

1 To make the salsa, drain the canned pineapple, reserving 2 tablespoons of the juice. Finely chop the pineapple flesh.

2 Place the pineapple, reserved juice, sugar, onion and chilli in a bowl and mix well. Leave to stand for at least 1 hour for the flavours to develop fully.

3 Meanwhile, mix the mustard, paprika, ginger, nutmeg and sugar together in a bowl. Spread the mixture evenly over the skin of the duckling halves.

4 Barbecue the duckling skin-side up over hot coals for about 30 minutes.

Turn the duckling over and barbecue for 10–15 minutes or until the duckling is cooked through.

5 Serve with fresh salad leaves and the pineapple salsa.

COOK'S TIP
Place the duckling in a rectangular foil tray to protect the delicate flesh on the barbecue.

Boozy Beef Steaks

A simple marinade gives plain barbecued steaks a fabulous flavour in return for very little effort in the kitchen.

NUTRITIONAL INFORMATION

Calories 371	Sugars 5g	
Protein 48g	Fat 14g	
Carbohydrate 6g	Saturates 6g	

2 mins, plus 2 hrs marinating   15–25 mins

SERVES 4

I N G R E D I E N T S

4 beef steaks

4 tbsp whisky or brandy

2 tbsp soy sauce

1 tbsp dark muscovado sugar

pepper

fresh sprig of parsley, to garnish

T O   S E R V E

garlic bread

slices of tomato

1 Make a few cuts in the edge of the fat on each steak. This will stop the meat curling as it cooks.

2 Place the beef steaks in a shallow, non-metallic dish.

3 Combine the whisky or brandy, soy sauce, sugar and pepper to taste in a bowl, stirring until the sugar dissolves. Pour the mixture over the steak. Cover and leave to marinate for at least 2 hours.

4 Barbecue the meat over hot coals, searing the meat over the hottest part of the barbecue for about 2 minutes on each side.

5 Move the meat to an area with slightly less intense heat and cook for a further 4–10 minutes on each side, depending on how well done you like your steaks. Test the meat is cooked by inserting the tip of a knife – the juices will run from red when the meat is still rare, to clear as it becomes well cooked.

6 Lightly barbecue the slices of tomato for 1–2 minutes.

7 Transfer the meat and the tomatoes to warm plates. Garnish with a sprig of parsley and serve with garlic bread.

Lamb with a Spice Crust

Lamb neck fillet is a tender cut that is not too thick and is, therefore, ideal for cooking on the barbecue.

NUTRITIONAL INFORMATION

Calories 203   Sugars 9g
Protein . . . . .16g   Fat 10g
Carbohydrate . . .12g   Saturates 4g

 5 mins   40–45 mins

SERVES 4

I N G R E D I E N T S

1 tbsp olive oil

2 tbsp light muscovado sugar

2 tbsp wholegrain mustard

1 tbsp horseradish sauce

1 tbsp plain flour

350 g/12 oz neck fillet of lamb

salt and pepper

TO SERVE

coleslaw

slices of tomato

1 Combine the oil, sugar, mustard, horseradish sauce, flour and salt and pepper to taste in a shallow, non-metallic dish until they are well mixed.

2 Roll the lamb in the spice mixture until well coated.

3 Lightly oil one or two pieces of foil or a large, double thickness of foil. Place the lamb on the foil and wrap it up so that the meat is completely enclosed.

4 Place the foil parcel over hot coals for 30 minutes, turning the parcel over occasionally to cook evenly.

5 Carefully open the foil parcel, spoon the cooking juices over the spiced lamb and continue to barbecue for a further 10–15 minutes, or until completely cooked through.

6 Place the lamb on a platter and remove the foil. Cut into thick slices and serve with coleslaw and tomato slices.

COOK'S TIP

If preferred, the lamb can be completely removed from the kitchen foil for the second part of the cooking. Barbecue the lamb directly over the coals for a smokier barbecue flavour, basting with extra oil if necessary.

Butterfly Lamb with Mint

The appearance of the leg of lamb as it is opened out to cook on the barbecue gives this dish its name.

NUTRITIONAL INFORMATION

Calories . . . . . . .733 Sugars 6g
Protein . . . . .69g Fat 48g
Carbohydrate . . . .6g Saturates 13g

10 mins, plus 6 hrs marinating   1 hr

SERVES 4

INGREDIENTS

boned leg of lamb, about 1.8 kg/4 lb

8 tbsp balsamic vinegar

grated rind and juice of 1 lemon

150 ml/5 fl oz sunflower oil

4 tbsp chopped fresh mint

2 cloves garlic, crushed

2 tbsp light muscovado sugar

salt and pepper

TO SERVE

grilled vegetables

green salad leaves

1 Open out the boned leg of lamb so that its shape resembles a butterfly. Thread 2–3 skewers through the meat to make it easier to turn on the barbecue.

2 Combine the balsamic vinegar, lemon rind and juice, oil, mint, garlic, sugar and seasoning to taste in a non-metallic dish large enough to hold the lamb.

3 Place the lamb in the dish and turn it over a few times so that the meat is coated on both sides with the marinade. Leave to marinate for at least 6 hours or preferably overnight, turning occasionally.

4 Remove the lamb from the marinade and reserve the liquid for basting.

5 Place the rack about 15 cm/6 inches above the coals and barbecue the lamb for about 30 minutes on each side, turning once and basting frequently with the marinade.

6 Transfer the lamb to a chopping board and remove the skewers. Cut the lamb into slices across the grain and serve with grilled vegetables and green salad leaves.

Ham Steaks with Apple

This dish is quick to prepare because there is no marinating involved. Ham has a good, strong flavour and cooks well on the barbecue.

NUTRITIONAL INFORMATION

Calories ....358 Sugars 13g
Protein ....31g Fat 21g
Carbohydrate ...13g Saturates 8g

5 mins   9–12 mins

SERVES 4

INGREDIENTS

4 ham steaks, each about 175 g/6 oz

1–2 tsp wholegrain mustard

1 tbsp honey

2 tbsp lemon juice

1 tbsp sunflower oil

APPLE RINGS

2 green dessert apples

2 tsp demerara sugar

¼ tsp ground nutmeg

¼ tsp ground cinnamon

¼ tsp ground allspice

1–2 tbsp melted butter

1   Using a pair of scissors, make a few cuts around the edges of the ham steaks to prevent them from curling up as they cook. Spread a little wholegrain mustard over the steaks.

2   Mix together the honey, lemon juice and oil in a bowl.

3   To prepare the apple rings, core the apples and cut them into thick slices. Mix the sugar with the spices and press the apple slices in the mixture until well coated on both sides.

4   Barbecue the steaks over hot coals for 3–4 minutes on each side, basting with the honey and lemon mixture to prevent them drying out during cooking.

5   Brush the apple slices with a little melted butter and barbecue alongside the pork for 3–4 minutes, turning once and brushing with melted butter as they cook.

6   Serve the ham steaks garnished with the apple slices.

COOK'S TIP

Ham can be a little salty. If you have time, soak the steaks in cold water for 30–60 minutes before cooking – this process will remove the excess salt.

Tangy Pork Fillet

Barbecued in a parcel of kitchen foil, these tasty pork fillets are served with a tangy orange sauce.

NUTRITIONAL INFORMATION

Calories	.......230g	Sugars	........16g
Protein	........19g	Fat	...........9g
Carbohydrate	...20g	Saturates	.......3g

 10 mins   55 mins

SERVES 4

INGREDIENTS

400 g/14 oz lean pork fillet

3 tbsp orange marmalade

grated rind and juice of 1 orange

1 tbsp white wine vinegar

dash of Tabasco sauce

salt and pepper

SAUCE

1 tbsp olive oil

1 small onion, chopped

1 small green pepper, deseeded and thinly sliced

1 tbsp cornflour

150 ml/5 fl oz orange juice

TO SERVE

cooked rice

mixed salad leaves

1 Place a large piece of double thickness foil in a shallow dish. Put the pork fillet in the centre of the foil and season to taste.

2 Heat the marmalade, orange rind and juice, vinegar and Tabasco sauce in a small pan, stirring until the marmalade melts and the ingredients combine. Pour the mixture over the pork and wrap the meat in the foil. Seal the parcel well so that the juices cannot run out. Place over hot coals and barbecue for about 25 minutes, turning the parcel occasionally.

3 For the sauce, heat the oil and cook the onion for 2–3 minutes. Add the pepper and cook for 3–4 minutes.

4 Remove the pork from the kitchen foil and place on to the rack. Pour the juices into the pan with the sauce.

5 Barbecue the pork for a further 10–20 minutes, turning, until cooked through and golden on the outside.

6 In a bowl, mix the cornflour with a little orange juice to form a paste. Add to the sauce with the remaining cooking juices and cook, stirring, until it thickens. Slice the pork, spoon over the sauce and serve with rice and salad leaves.

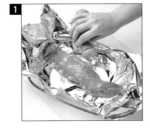  

Sticky Chicken Drumsticks

These drumsticks are always popular – provide plenty of napkins for wiping sticky fingers, or finger bowls with a slice of lemon.

NUTRITIONAL INFORMATION

Calories 213   Sugars 14g
Protein . . . . .27g   Fat 6g
Carbohydrate . . .14g   Saturates 2g

5 mins   30 mins

SERVES 4

INGREDIENTS

10 chicken drumsticks

4 tbsp fine-cut orange marmalade

1 tbsp Worcestershire sauce

grated rind and juice of ½ orange

salt and pepper

TO SERVE

cherry tomatoes

salad leaves

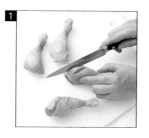

1 Make 2–3 slashes in the flesh of each of the chicken drumsticks with a sharp knife.

2 Bring a large saucepan of water to the boil and add the chicken drumsticks. Cover the pan, return to the boil and cook for 5–10 minutes. Remove the chicken and drain thoroughly.

3 Meanwhile, make the baste. Place the orange marmalade, Worcestershire sauce, orange rind and juice and salt and pepper to taste in a small saucepan. Heat gently, stirring continuously, until the marmalade melts and the ingredients are well combined.

4 Brush the baste over the par-cooked chicken drumsticks and transfer to the barbecue to finish cooking. Cook the drumsticks over hot coals for about 10 minutes, turning and basting the meat frequently with the remaining baste.

5 Carefully thread 3 cherry tomatoes on to a skewer per person and transfer to the barbecue for 1–2 minutes.

6 Transfer the chicken drumsticks to serving plates. Serve with the cherry tomato skewers and a selection of fresh salad leaves.

COOK'S TIP

Par-cooking the chicken is an ideal way of making sure that it is cooked all the way through without becoming overcooked and burned on the outside.

Filipino Chicken

Tomato ketchup is a very popular ingredient in Asian dishes, as it imparts a zingy sweet-sour flavour.

NUTRITIONAL INFORMATION

Calories 197	Sugars 7g
Protein 28g	Fat 4g
Carbohydrate 8g	Saturates 1g

10 mins, plus 2¹/₂ hrs marinating   20 mins

SERVES 4

I N G R E D I E N T S

1 can lemonade or lime-and-lemonade

2 tbsp gin

4 tbsp tomato ketchup

2 tsp garlic salt

2 tsp Worcestershire sauce

4 lean chicken suprêmes or breast fillets

salt and pepper

TO SERVE

thread egg noodles

1 green chilli, chopped finely

2 spring onions, sliced

1 Combine the lemonade or lime-and-lemonade, gin, tomato ketchup, garlic salt, Worcestershire sauce and seasoning in a large, non-porous dish.

2 Put the chicken suprêmes into the dish and make sure that the marinade covers them completely.

3 Leave the meat to marinate in the refrigerator for 2 hours, then remove and leave covered at room temperature for 30 minutes.

4 Place the chicken over a medium-hot barbecue and cook for 20 minutes, turning the chicken once, halfway through the cooking time.

5 Remove the cooked meat from the barbecue and leave to rest for 3–4 minutes before serving.

6 Serve with egg noodles, tossed with a little green chilli and spring onions.

Grilled Chicken & Vegetables

Grilling is a quick, healthy cooking method, ideal for sealing in the juices of chicken breasts, and a wonderful way to cook summer vegetables.

NUTRITIONAL INFORMATION

Calories . . . . .611 Sugars 11g
Protein . . . . .43g Fat 21g
Carbohydrate . . .66g Saturates 3g

5 mins, plus
1 hr draining/
marinating   25 mins

SERVES 4

INGREDIENTS

1 small aubergine, sliced

2 garlic cloves, crushed

finely grated rind of ½ lemon

1 tbsp chopped fresh mint

6 tbsp olive oil

4 boneless chicken breasts

2 medium courgettes, sliced

1 medium red pepper, quartered

1 small bulb fennel, sliced thickly

1 large red onion, sliced thickly

1 small ciabatta loaf, or
  1 French baguette, sliced

extra olive oil

salt and pepper

1 Place the aubergine slices in a colander and sprinkle with salt. Leave over a bowl to drain for about 30 minutes, then rinse and dry. This will draw out all of the bitter juices.

2 Mix together the garlic, lemon rind, mint and olive oil, and season.

3 Slash the chicken breasts at intervals with a sharp knife. Spoon over about half of the oil mixture and stir to combine.

4 Combine the aubergines and the remaining vegetables. Toss in the remaining oil mixture. Leave the chicken and vegetables to marinate for about 30 minutes.

5 Place the chicken breasts and vegetables on a preheated hot grill or barbecue for about 20 minutes, turning occasionally, until they are golden brown and tender, or cook on a ridged griddle pan on the hob.

6 Brush the bread slices with olive oil and grill until golden.

7 Drizzle a little olive oil over the chicken and grilled vegetables and serve hot or cold with the toasts.

Chicken with Lime & Mint

These tangy lime-and-honey-coated chicken pieces have a matching sauce or dip based on creamy natural yogurt.

NUTRITIONAL INFORMATION

Calories . . . . .170 Sugars 12g

Protein . . . . .23g Fat 3g

Carbohydrate . . .12g Saturates 1g

  5 mins, plus 30 mins marinating 20 mins

SERVES 4–6

INGREDIENTS

3 tbsp finely chopped mint

4 tbsp clear honey

4 tbsp lime juice

12 boneless chicken thighs

SAUCE

150 ml/5 fl oz natural thick yogurt

1 tbsp finely chopped mint

2 tsp finely grated lime rind

VARIATION

Use this marinade for chicken kebabs, alternating the chicken with lime and red onion wedges.

1 Combine the mint, honey and lime juice in a bowl.

2 Use cocktail sticks to keep the chicken thighs in neat shapes and add the chicken to the marinade, turning to coat evenly.

3 Leave to marinate for at least 30 minutes, preferably overnight. Cook the chicken on a preheated medium-hot barbecue or grill, turning frequently and basting with the marinade. The chicken is cooked if the juices run clear when the meat is pierced in the thickest part with a skewer.

4 Meanwhile, mix the sauce ingredients together in a small bowl.

5 Remove the cocktail sticks and serve the chicken with salad and the sauce.

Skewered Chicken Spirals

These unusual chicken kebabs have a wonderful Italian flavour, and the bacon helps keep them moist during cooking.

NUTRITIONAL INFORMATION

Calories 231   Sugars 1g
Protein . . . . .29g   Fat 13g
Carbohydrate . . . .1g   Saturates 5g

 15 mins   10 mins

SERVES 4

I N G R E D I E N T S

4 chicken breasts, skinned and boned

1 garlic clove, crushed

2 tbsp tomato purée

4 slices smoked back bacon

large handful of fresh basil leaves

oil for brushing

salt and pepper

green salad, to serve

1 Spread out a piece of chicken between two sheets of clingfilm and beat firmly with a rolling pin to flatten the meat to an even thickness. Repeat with the remaining chicken breasts.

2 Mix the garlic and tomato purée and spread over the chicken. Lay a bacon slice over each, then scatter with the basil. Season with salt and pepper.

3 Roll up each piece of chicken firmly, then cut into thick slices.

4 Thread the slices on to 4 skewers, making sure the skewer holds the chicken in a spiral shape.

5 Brush lightly with oil and cook on a preheated hot barbecue or grill for about 10 minutes, turning once. Serve hot with a green salad.

  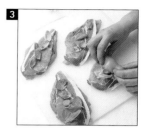

Tequila Chicken Wings

Tequila tenderizes these tasty chicken wings. Serve accompanied by corn tortillas, refried beans, salsa and lots of chilled lager.

NUTRITIONAL INFORMATION

Calories 489	Sugars 8g
Protein 41g	Fat 30g
Carbohydrate 11g	Saturates 7g

5 mins, plus 3 hrs marinating   15–20 mins

SERVES 4

I N G R E D I E N T S

900 g/2 lb chicken wings

11 garlic cloves, finely chopped

juice of 2 limes

juice of 1 orange

2 tbsp tequila

1 tbsp mild chilli powder

2 dried chipotle chillies, reconstituted and puréed

2 tbsp vegetable oil

1 tsp sugar

¼ tsp ground allspice

pinch of ground cinnamon

pinch of ground cumin

pinch of dried oregano

1 Cut the chicken wings into two pieces at the joint.

2 Combine the remaining ingredients thoroughly in a non-metallic dish. Add the chicken wings, toss well to coat, then leave in the refrigerator for at least 3 hours to marinate, or preferably overnight.

3 Cook the chicken over hot coals for about 15–20 minutes or until the wings are crisply browned, turning occasionally. To test whether the chicken is cooked, pierce a thick part with a skewer – the juices should run clear. Serve immediately.

COOK'S TIP

Made from the agave plant, tequila is Mexico's famous alcoholic drink.

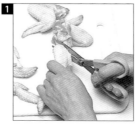

Lamb on Rosemary Skewers

Wild rosemary scents the air all over the Mediterranean – here, sprigs are used as skewers for succulent lamb cubes with Turkish flavourings.

NUTRITIONAL INFORMATION

Calories ....286 Sugars 5g
Protein ....27g Fat 16g
Carbohydrate ....7g Saturates 6g

10 mins, plus 4 hrs marinating   10–12 mins

MAKES 4

INGREDIENTS

500 g/1 lb 2 oz boneless leg of lamb

4 long, thick branches fresh rosemary

1 or 2 red peppers, depending on the size

12 large garlic cloves, peeled

olive oil

Spiced Pilau with Saffron (see page 71), to serve

MARINADE

2 tbsp olive oil

2 tbsp dry white wine

½ tsp ground cumin

1 sprig fresh oregano, chopped

1 Cut the lamb into 5 cm/2 inch cubes. Mix the marinade ingredients in a bowl. Add the lamb, stir well to coat and leave to marinate for 4–12 hours.

2 An hour before cooking, put the rosemary in a bowl of cold water and leave to soak.

3 Slice the tops off the peppers, cut into quarters, and remove the cores and seeds. Cut the quarters into 5 cm/ 2 inch pieces.

4 Bring a small pan of water to the boil, blanch the pepper pieces and garlic cloves for 1 minute. Drain and refresh under cold water. Pat dry and set aside.

5 Drain the rosemary and pat dry. Remove the needles from the first 4 cm/1¾ inches of the branches to make a handle for turning while grilling.

6 Thread alternate pieces of lamb, garlic and pepper on to the herb skewers: the meat should be tender enough to push the sprig through it. If not, use a metal skewer to poke a hole through each cube.

7 Lightly oil the barbecue rack. Place the skewers on the rack, 12.5 cm/ 5 inches away from the heat source, and cook for 10–12 minutes, brushing with leftover marinade or oil and turning, until the meat is cooked. Serve with the pilau.

Beef Satay

Satay recipes vary throughout the East, but these little beef skewers are a classic version of the traditional dish.

NUTRITIONAL INFORMATION

Calories 489	Sugars 14g	
Protein 38g	Fat 31g	
Carbohydrate ...17g	Saturates 8g	

5 mins, plus 2 hrs marinating   3–5 mins

SERVES 4

INGREDIENTS

500 g/1 lb 2 oz beef fillet

2 garlic cloves, crushed

1½ tsp finely grated fresh ginger root

1 tbsp soft light brown sugar

1 tbsp dark soy sauce

1 tbsp lime juice

2 tsp sesame oil

1 tsp ground coriander

1 tsp turmeric

½ tsp chilli powder

chopped cucumber and red pepper, to serve

PEANUT SAUCE

300 ml/10 fl oz coconut milk

8 tbsp crunchy peanut butter

½ small onion, grated

2 tsp soft light brown sugar

½ tsp chilli powder

1 tbsp dark soy sauce

1 Cut the beef into 1 cm/½ inch cubes and place in a large bowl.

2 Add the crushed garlic, grated ginger, sugar, soy sauce, lime juice, sesame oil, ground coriander, turmeric and chilli powder. Mix together well to coat the pieces of meat evenly. Cover and leave to marinate in the refrigerator for at least 2 hours, or overnight.

3 For the peanut sauce, place all the ingredients in a pan and stir over a medium heat until boiling. Remove from the heat and keep warm.

4 Soak the skewers for 20 minutes. Thread with the beef. Barbecue or cook under a preheated grill for 3–5 minutes, turning often. Serve with the sauce, cucumber and red pepper.

Blackened Fish

The word 'blackened' refers to the spicy marinade used to coat the fish, which chars as it cooks. Choose a firm-textured fish such as halibut.

NUTRITIONAL INFORMATION

Calories . . . . .331 Sugars 0g
Protein . . . . .37g Fat 20g
Carbohydrate . . .0.1g Saturates 8g

 5 mins   20 mins

SERVES 4

I N G R E D I E N T S

4 white fish steaks
1 tbsp paprika
1 tsp dried thyme
1 tsp cayenne pepper
1 tsp freshly ground black pepper
½ tsp freshly ground white pepper
½ tsp salt
¼ tsp ground allspice
4 tbsp unsalted butter
3 tbsp sunflower oil

1 Rinse the fish steaks and pat them dry with absorbent kitchen paper.

2 Mix together the paprika, dried thyme, cayenne pepper, black and white peppers, salt and allspice in a shallow dish.

3 Place the butter and oil in a small pan and heat, stirring occasionally, until the butter melts.

4 Brush the butter mixture liberally all over the fish steaks, on both sides.

5 Dip the fish into the spicy mix until well coated on both sides.

6 Barbecue the fish over hot coals for about 10 minutes on each side, turning once. Continue to baste the fish with the remaining butter mixture during the cooking time.

VARIATION

A whole fish – red mullet, for example – rather than steaks is also delicious cooked this way. The spicy seasoning can also be used to coat chicken portions, if you prefer.

Char-grilled Bream

Bream have a good, firm flesh and so are easy to grill. They do not need elaborate accompaniments to make a tasty meal.

NUTRITIONAL INFORMATION

Calories 397	Sugars 1g
Protein 35g	Fat 28g
Carbohydrate 1g	Saturates 3g

 5 mins   20–30 mins

SERVES 2

I N G R E D I E N T S

2 small sea bream, scaled, gutted,
    trimmed and cleaned

2 slices lemon

2 bay leaves

salt and pepper

B A S T E

4 tbsp olive oil

2 tbsp lemon juice

½ tsp chopped fresh oregano

½ tsp chopped fresh thyme

T O   G A R N I S H

fresh bay leaves

fresh thyme sprig

lemon wedges

1 Using a sharp knife, cut 2–3 deep slashes into the bodies of both fish in order to help them fully absorb the flavour of the basting sauce.

2 Place a slice of lemon and a bay leaf inside the cavity of each fish. Season inside the cavity with salt and pepper to taste.

3 In a small bowl, mix together the ingredients for the baste using a fork. Alternatively, place all the basting ingredients in a small screw-top jar and shake well to combine.

4 Brush some of the lemon and herb baste liberally over the fish and place them on a barbecue rack over hot coals. Barbecue for 20–30 minutes, turning and basting the fish frequently.

5 Transfer to a serving plate, garnish with fresh bay leaves, thyme and lemon wedges and serve.

COOK'S TIP

The flavour of the dish will be enhanced if you use good fresh ingredients in the sauce. The flavour of dried herbs is much more intense, so only use half the quantity of the fresh herbs listed above.

Salmon Brochettes

These tasty kebabs have a lovely summery flavour. Serve on a bread croûte with fresh tomato sauce.

NUTRITIONAL INFORMATION

Calories 535   Sugars 7g
Protein . . . . .26g   Fat 42g
Carbohydrate . . .14g   Saturates 7g

 5–10 mins, plus 15 mins chilling   10 mins

SERVES 4

I N G R E D I E N T S

450 g/1 lb salmon, skinned and cut into large chunks

1 tbsp cornflour

½ tsp salt

½ tsp pepper

1 small egg white, beaten

1 red pepper, deseeded and cut into chunks

1 green pepper, deseeded and cut into chunks

4 tbsp olive oil

ciabatta bread, to serve

T O M A T O   S A U C E

4 tomatoes, deseeded and quartered

¼ cucumber, peeled, deseeded and chopped

8 fresh basil leaves

6 tbsp olive oil

2 tbsp lemon juice

salt and pepper

1 Place the salmon in a shallow dish and sprinkle over the cornflour and salt and pepper. Add the beaten egg white and toss well to coat. Leave to chill for 15 minutes.

2 Thread the pieces of salmon on to 4 skewers, alternating the fish pieces with the chunks of red and green peppers. Set the skewers aside while you make the tomato sauce.

3 To make the sauce, place all of the ingredients in a food processor and chop coarsely. Alternatively, chop the tomatoes, cucumber and basil leaves by hand and mix with the oil, lemon juice and seasoning. Leave to chill.

4 Barbecue the salmon brochettes over hot coals for 10 minutes, brushing frequently with olive oil to prevent them from drying during cooking.

5 Cut the ciabatta bread at an angle to produce 4 long slices. Lightly toast on the barbecue.

6 To serve, spread the sauce over each slice of bread and top with a salmon brochette.

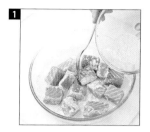

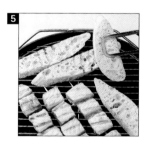

Mackerel with Lime

The secret of this dish lies in the simple, fresh flavours which perfectly complement the fish.

NUTRITIONAL INFORMATION

Calories	302	Sugars 0g
Protein	........21g	Fat 24g
Carbohydrate	....0g	Saturates 4g

10 mins   10 mins

SERVES 4

INGREDIENTS

4 small mackerel

¼ tsp ground coriander

¼ tsp ground cumin

4 tbsp chopped fresh coriander

1 red chilli, deseeded and chopped

grated rind and juice of 1 lime

2 tbsp sunflower oil

salt and pepper

salad leaves, to serve

TO GARNISH

1 lime, sliced

4 small red chillies, for flowers (optional)

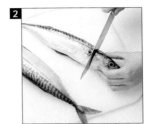

1 To make the chilli flowers (if using), cut the tip of each small red chilli lengthways into thin strips, leaving the chilli intact at the stem end. Remove the seeds and place the chilli in iced water until it has curled.

2 Clean and gut the mackerel, removing the heads if preferred. Transfer the mackerel to a chopping board.

3 Sprinkle the fish with the ground spices and salt and pepper to taste. Sprinkle 1 teaspoon of chopped coriander inside the cavity of each fish.

4 Mix together the rest of the chopped coriander, chilli, lime rind and juice and the oil in a small bowl. Brush the mixture liberally over the fish.

5 Place the fish in a hinged rack if you have one. Barbecue the fish over hot coals for 3–4 minutes on each side, turning once and brushing frequently with the remaining baste.

6 Transfer the fish to plates, garnish with chilli flowers (if using) and lime slices, and serve with salad leaves.

Nutty Stuffed Trout

Stuff the trout just before cooking. If you prefer, the fish can be cooked in foil parcels on the barbecue.

NUTRITIONAL INFORMATION

Calories	356	Sugars	.........2g
Protein	........40g	Fat	..........17g
Carbohydrate	....11g	Saturates	.......3g

 5 mins   22 mins

SERVES 4

I N G R E D I E N T S

4 medium trout, gutted and cleaned

2 tbsp sunflower oil

1 small onion, finely chopped

50 g/1¾ oz toasted mixed nuts, chopped

grated rind of 1 orange

2 tbsp orange juice

75 g/2¾ oz fresh wholemeal breadcrumbs

1 medium egg, beaten

oil for brushing

salt and pepper

orange slices, to garnish

orange and watercress salad, to serve

1 Season the trout inside and out with salt and pepper.

2 To make the stuffing, heat the oil in a small pan and fry the onion until soft. Remove from the heat and stir in the chopped nuts, grated orange rind, orange juice and breadcrumbs. Add just enough beaten egg to bind the mixture together.

3 Divide the stuffing into 4 equal portions and spoon into the body of each fish.

4 Brush the fish liberally with oil and barbecue over medium hot coals for 10 minutes on each side, turning once.

When the fish is cooked the flesh will be white and firm and the skin will be beginning to crispen.

5 Transfer the fish to individual serving plates and garnish with orange slices.

6 Serve the stuffed trout with an orange and watercress salad drizzled with an orange and mustard dressing (see Cook's Tip, right).

COOK'S TIP

For an orange and mustard dressing, mix together 2 tablespoons of orange juice, 1 tablespoon of white wine vinegar, 3 tablespoons of olive oil, ½ teaspoon of wholegrain mustard, and salt and pepper to taste.

Herrings with Tarragon

The fish are filled with an orange-flavoured stuffing and are wrapped in kitchen foil before being baked on the barbecue.

NUTRITIONAL INFORMATION

Calories 332   Sugars 4g

Protein . . . . .21g   Fat 24g

Carbohydrate . . . .9g   Saturates 6g

 15 mins   35 mins

SERVES 4

I N G R E D I E N T S

1 orange

4 spring onions

50 g/1¾ oz fresh wholemeal breadcrumbs

1 tbsp chopped fresh tarragon

4 herrings, gutted and cleaned

salt and pepper

green salad, to serve

T O   G A R N I S H

2 oranges

1 tbsp light brown sugar

1 tbsp olive oil

sprigs of fresh tarragon

1 Pare the rind from half of the orange, using a zester.

2 Peel and chop all of the orange flesh on a plate, to catch all of the juice.

3 Mix together the orange flesh, juice, rind, spring onions, breadcrumbs and tarragon in a bowl. Season with salt and pepper to taste.

4 Divide the stuffing into 4 equal portions and use it to fill the body cavities of the fish.

5 Place each fish on to a square of lightly greased foil and wrap the foil around them to enclose them completely. Barbecue over hot coals for 20–30 minutes until cooked through – the flesh should be white and firm to the touch.

6 Meanwhile make the garnish. Peel and thickly slice the 2 oranges and sprinkle over the sugar.

7 Just before the fish is cooked, drizzle a little oil over the orange slices and barbecue for 5 minutes to heat through.

8 Transfer the fish to serving plates and garnish with the barbecued orange slices and sprigs of fresh tarragon.

9 Serve the stuffed herrings with a fresh green salad.

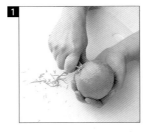

Herb & Garlic Prawns

A rich garlic and herb butter coats these skewered prawns, and cooking on a barbecue really brings out their flavour.

NUTRITIONAL INFORMATION

Calories	150	Sugars 0g
Protein	. . . . .16g	Fat 9g
Carbohydrate	. . . .1g	Saturates 5g

5 mins, plus 30 mins marinating

7–12 mins

SERVES 4

I N G R E D I E N T S

350 g/12 oz raw prawns, peeled

2 tbsp chopped fresh parsley

4 tbsp lemon juice

2 tbsp olive oil

5 tbsp butter

2 cloves garlic, chopped

salt and pepper

1 Place the prepared prawns in a shallow, non-metallic dish with the parsley, lemon juice and salt and pepper to taste. Leave the prawns to marinate in the herb mixture for at least 30 minutes.

2 Heat the oil and butter in a small pan with the garlic until the butter melts. Stir to mix thoroughly.

3 Remove the prawns from the marinade with a perforated spoon and add them to the pan containing the garlic butter. Stir the prawns into the garlic butter until well coated, then thread on to skewers.

4 Barbecue the kebabs over hot coals for 5–10 minutes, turning the skewers occasionally, until the prawns turn pink and are cooked through. Brush the prawns with the remaining garlic butter during the cooking time.

5 Transfer the prawn kebabs to serving plates. Drizzle over any remaining garlic butter and serve at once.

VARIATION

If raw prawns are unavailable, use cooked prawns but reduce the cooking time. Small cooked prawns can be prepared in a foil parcel instead of on skewers. Marinate them in the garlic butter, wrap in foil and cook for 5 minutes, shaking the parcels once or twice.

Stuffed Mackerel

This is a simple variation of a difficult Middle Eastern recipe which involves removing the fish flesh and reserving and re-stuffing the skin.

NUTRITIONAL INFORMATION

Calories 488	Sugars 12g
Protein 34g	Fat 34g
Carbohydrate ...12g	Saturates 6g

 5 mins   16 mins

SERVES 4

INGREDIENTS

4 large mackerel, gutted and cleaned

1 tbsp olive oil

1 small onion, finely sliced

1 tsp ground cinnamon

½ tsp ground ginger

2 tbsp raisins

2 tbsp pine kernels, toasted

8 vine leaves in brine, drained

salt and pepper

VARIATION

This simple, easy-to-make pine kernel stuffing works equally well with many other types of fish, including sea bass and red mullet.

1 Wash and dry the mackerel and set aside. Heat the oil in a small frying pan and add the onion. Cook gently for 5 minutes until softened. Add the ground cinnamon and ginger and cook for 30 seconds before adding the raisins and pine kernels. Remove from the heat and allow to cool.

2 Stuff each of the fish with a quarter of the onion and pine kernel mixture.

Wrap each stuffed fish in 2 vine leaves, securing them with cocktail sticks.

3 Cook on a preheated barbecue or ridged grill pan for 5 minutes on each side, until the vine leaves have scorched and the fish is tender. Serve immediately.

Swordfish Steaks

Salsa verde is a classic Italian sauce of herbs, garlic and anchovies.
It simply means 'green sauce'.

NUTRITIONAL INFORMATION

Calories	548	Sugars	.......0.1g
Protein	........28g	Fat	..........48g
Carbohydrate	....1g	Saturates	.......7g

5 mins, plus 2 hrs marinating

4–6 mins

SERVES 4

INGREDIENTS

4 swordfish steaks, about
 150 g/5½ oz each

4 tbsp olive oil

1 garlic clove, crushed

1 tsp lemon rind

SALSA VERDE

25 g/1 oz flat leaf parsley leaves

15 g/½ oz mixed herbs, such as basil, mint
 and chives

1 garlic clove, chopped

1 tbsp capers, drained and rinsed

1 tbsp green peppercorns in brine, drained

4 anchovies in oil, drained and
 roughly chopped

1 tsp Dijon mustard

125 ml/4 fl oz extra virgin olive oil

salt and pepper

1 Wash and dry the swordfish steaks and arrange them in a non-metallic dish. Mix together the olive oil, garlic and lemon rind, then pour the mixture over the swordfish steaks and leave them to marinate for at least 2 hours.

2 For the salsa verde, put the parsley leaves, mixed herbs, garlic, capers, green peppercorns, anchovies, mustard and olive oil into a food processor or blender. Blend to a smooth paste, adding a little warm water if necessary. Season to taste and set aside.

3 Remove the swordfish steaks from the marinade. Cook on a barbecue or preheated ridged grill pan for 2–3 minutes each side until tender. Serve immediately with the salsa verde.

VARIATION

Any firm-fleshed fish will work well in this recipe and absorb the classic Italian flavours. Try using tuna, or even shark steaks.

Barbecued Monkfish

Monkfish is an ideal fish for a barbecue because of its firm flesh, which stays solid on the skewers as it cooks.

NUTRITIONAL INFORMATION

Calories 219	Sugars 0.1g	
Protein 28g	Fat 12g	
Carbohydrate 1g	Saturates 2g	

5 mins, plus
2 hrs marinat-
ing/soaking   5–6 mins

SERVES 4

INGREDIENTS

4 tbsp olive oil

grated rind of 1 lime

2 tsp Thai fish sauce

2 garlic cloves, crushed

1 tsp grated fresh ginger root

2 tbsp chopped fresh basil

700 g/1 lb 9 oz monkfish fillet,
  cut into chunks

2 limes, each cut into 6 wedges

salt and pepper

1 Mix together the olive oil, lime rind, fish sauce, garlic, ginger and basil. Season and set aside.

2 Wash the monkfish chunks and pat dry. Add the chunks to the marinade and mix well. Leave to marinate for 2 hours, stirring occasionally.

3 If you are using bamboo skewers, soak them in cold water for 30 minutes. Then, lift the monkfish pieces from the marinade and thread them on to the skewers, alternating with the lime wedges.

4 Transfer the skewers, either to a barbecue or to a preheated ridged grill pan. Cook for 5–6 minutes, turning regularly, until the fish is tender. Serve immediately.

VARIATION

You could use any other white-fleshed fish for this recipe but sprinkle the pieces with salt and leave for 2 hours to firm the flesh, before rinsing, drying and then adding to the marinade.

Mixed Seafood Brochettes

If your fishmonger sells turbot in steaks, you will probably need one large steak for this dish, cut into chunks.

NUTRITIONAL INFORMATION

Calories	455	Sugars	.......0.1g
Protein	........32g	Fat	..........20g
Carbohydrate	...39g	Saturates	.......9g

10 mins, plus 2 hrs marinating   20 mins

SERVES 4

INGREDIENTS

225 g/8 oz skinless, boneless turbot fillet

225 g/8 oz skinless, boneless salmon fillet

8 scallops

8 large tiger prawns or langoustines

16 fresh bay leaves

1 lemon, sliced

4 tbsp olive oil

grated rind of 1 lemon

4 tbsp chopped mixed herbs such as thyme, parsley, chives and basil

black pepper

LEMON BUTTER RICE

175 g/6 oz long-grain rice

grated rind and juice of 1 lemon

4 tbsp butter

salt and pepper

TO GARNISH

lemon wedges

dill sprigs

1 Chop the turbot and salmon fillets into 8 pieces each. Thread on to 8 skewers, with the scallops and tiger prawns or langoustines, alternating with the bay leaves and lemon slices. Put into a non-metallic dish in a single layer.

2 Mix together the olive oil, lemon rind, herbs and black pepper. Pour the mixture over the fish. Cover and leave to marinate for 2 hours, turning once or twice.

3 For the lemon butter rice, bring a large pan of salted water to the boil and add the rice and lemon rind. Return to the boil and simmer for 7–8 minutes until the rice is tender. Drain well and immediately stir in the lemon juice and butter. Season with salt and pepper to taste.

4 Meanwhile, lift the fish brochettes from their marinade and cook on a lit barbecue, under a preheated hot grill or in a preheated ridged grill pan for 8–10 minutes, turning regularly, until cooked through. Serve with lemon butter rice. Garnish with lemon wedges and dill.

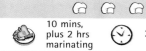

Char-grilled Scallops

Marinated scallops are char-grilled and served with couscous studded with colourful vegetables and herbs.

NUTRITIONAL INFORMATION

Calories 401	Sugars 3g	
Protein 20g	Fat 21g	
Carbohydrate . . .34g	Saturates 3g	

40 mins, plus 2 hrs marinating

12–13 mins

SERVES 4

INGREDIENTS

16 king scallops

3 tbsp olive oil

grated rind of 1 lime

2 tbsp chopped fresh basil

2 tbsp chopped fresh chives

1 garlic clove, finely chopped

black pepper

JEWELLED COUSCOUS

225 g/8 oz couscous

½ yellow pepper, deseeded and halved

½ red pepper, deseeded and halved

4 tbsp extra virgin olive oil

115 g/4 oz cucumber, chopped into 1 cm/½ inch pieces

3 spring onions, finely chopped

1 tbsp lime juice

2 tbsp shredded fresh basil

salt and pepper

TO GARNISH

basil leaves

lime wedges

1 Clean and trim the scallops. Put into a non-metallic dish. Mix together the olive oil, lime rind, basil, chives, garlic and black pepper. Pour over the scallops and cover. Leave to marinate for 2 hours.

2 Cook the couscous according to the packet instructions, omitting any butter recommended. Meanwhile, brush the pepper halves with olive oil and place under a preheated hot grill for 5–6 minutes, turning once, until the skins are blackened and the flesh is tender. Put into a plastic bag to cool. Peel off the skins and chop the flesh into 1 cm/½ inch pieces. Add to the couscous with the remaining oil, cucumber, spring onions, lemon juice and seasoning. Set aside.

3 Lift the scallops from the marinade and thread on to 4 skewers. Cook on a barbecue or preheated ridged grill pan for 1 minute on each side, until charred and firm but not quite cooked through. Remove from the heat and allow to rest for 2 minutes.

4 Stir the shredded basil into the couscous and divide on to plates. Put a skewer on each, garnished with basil leaves and lime wedges.

Tuna with Anchovy Butter

Meaty tuna has enough flavour to stand up to the robust taste of anchovies. Serve this with pan-fried potatoes or a mixed rice dish.

NUTRITIONAL INFORMATION

Calories 564	Sugars 0g
Protein 55g	Fat 38g
Carbohydrate 0g	Saturates 19g

5 mins, plus 15 mins chilling

8–16 mins

SERVES 4

INGREDIENTS

olive oil

4 thick tuna steaks, about 225 g/8 oz each, and 2 cm/¾ inch thick

ANCHOVY BUTTER

8 anchovy fillets in oil, drained

4 spring onions, finely chopped

1 tbsp finely grated orange rind

115 g/4 oz unsalted butter

¼ tsp lemon juice

pepper

TO GARNISH

fresh flat leaf parsley sprigs

orange rind strips

1 To make the anchovy butter, very finely chop the anchovies and put them in a bowl with the spring onions, orange rind and softened butter. Beat until all of the ingredients are blended well together, seasoning with lemon juice and pepper to taste.

2 Place the flavoured butter on a sheet of baking paper and roll up into a log shape. Fold over the ends and place in the freezer for 15 minutes to become firm.

3 Cook the tuna steaks for 2 minutes on an oiled barbecue rack over hot coals, or in an oiled, ridged griddle pan over a high heat, in batches if necessary. Turn the steaks over and cook for 2 minutes for rare, or up to 4 minutes for well done. Season to taste with salt and pepper.

4 Transfer the tuna steaks to warm serving plates and place 2 thin slices of anchovy butter on each steak. Garnish with parsley sprigs and strips of orange rind and serve at once.

VARIATION

If you like your food particularly hot and spicy, add a pinch of dried chilli flakes to the anchovy butter mixture for a little extra punch.

Fragrant Tuna Steaks

Fresh tuna steaks are very meaty – they have a firm texture, yet the flesh is succulent. Steaks from the belly are best of all.

NUTRITIONAL INFORMATION

Calories 239	Sugars 0.1g	
Protein 42g	Fat 8g	
Carbohydrate . . .0.5g	Saturates 2g	

15 mins   15 mins

SERVES 4

I N G R E D I E N T S

4 tuna steaks, about 175 g/6 oz each

½ tsp finely grated lime rind

1 garlic clove, crushed

2 tsp olive oil

1 tsp ground cumin

1 tsp ground coriander

pepper

1 tbsp lime juice

fresh coriander, to garnish

TO SERVE

avocado relish (see Cook's Tip, below)

lime wedges

tomato wedges

COOK'S TIP

For the avocado relish, peel and chop a small ripe avocado. Mix in 1 tablespoon of lime juice, 1 tablespoon of freshly chopped coriander, 1 small finely chopped red onion and some chopped fresh mango or tomato. Season to taste.

1 Trim the skin neatly from the tuna steaks, then rinse well and pat dry on absorbent kitchen paper.

2 In a small bowl, mix together the lime rind, garlic, olive oil, cumin, ground coriander and pepper to make a paste.

3 Spread the paste thinly on both sides of the tuna. Cook the tuna steaks for 5 minutes on both sides on a foil-covered barbecue rack over hot coals, or in an oiled, ridged griddle pan over a high heat, in batches if necessary. Check the steaks and cook for up to 5 minutes more, until they are cooked through, drain on kitchen paper, and transfer to a serving plate.

4 Sprinkle the lime juice and chopped coriander over the fish. Serve with avocado relish (see Cook's Tip), and tomato and lime wedges.

Bacon & Scallop Skewers

Wrapping bacon around the scallops helps to protect the delicate flesh from the intense heat and allows them to cook without becoming tough.

NUTRITIONAL INFORMATION

Calories 271	Sugars 6g
Protein 17g	Fat 20g
Carbohydrate 7g	Saturates 5g

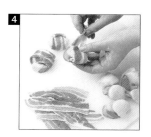

10 mins, plus 1–2 hrs marinating

5 mins

MAKES 4

INGREDIENTS

grated rind and juice of ½ lemon

4 tbsp sunflower oil

½ tsp dried dill

12 scallops

1 red pepper

1 green pepper

1 yellow pepper

6 rashers smoked streaky bacon

1 Mix together the lemon rind and juice, oil and dill in a non-metallic dish. Add the scallops and mix thoroughly to coat. Leave to marinate for 1–2 hours.

2 Cut the red, green and yellow peppers in half and deseed them. Cut the pepper halves into 2.5 cm/1 inch pieces and then set aside until required.

3 Remove the rind from the bacon. Stretch the rashers with the back of a knife, then cut each rasher in half.

4 Remove the scallops from the marinade, reserving any excess marinade. Wrap a piece of bacon firmly around each scallop.

5 Thread the bacon-wrapped scallops on to skewers, alternating with the pepper pieces.

6 Barbecue the bacon and scallop skewers over hot coals for about 5 minutes, basting frequently with the lemon and oil marinade.

7 Transfer the skewers to serving plates and serve immediately.

VARIATION
Peel 4–8 raw prawns and add them to the marinade with the scallops. Thread them on to the skewers alternately with the scallops and peppers.

Beef Tomato & Olive Kebabs

These kebabs have a Mediterranean flavour. The sweetness of the tomatoes and the sharpness of the olives makes them irresistible.

NUTRITIONAL INFORMATION

Calories	166	Sugars	.........1g
Protein	........12g	Fat	..........12g
Carbohydrate	....1g	Saturates	.......3g

   5 mins   10–17 mins

MAKES 8

I N G R E D I E N T S

450 g/1 lb rump or sirloin steak

16 cherry tomatoes

16 large stoned green olives

salt and freshly ground black pepper

focaccia bread, to serve

B A S T E

4 tbsp olive oil

1 tbsp sherry vinegar

1 clove garlic, crushed

F R E S H   T O M A T O   R E L I S H

1 tbsp olive oil

½ red onion, finely chopped

1 clove garlic, chopped

6 plum tomatoes, deseeded, skinned and chopped

2 pitted green olives, sliced

1 tbsp chopped fresh parsley

1 tbsp lemon juice

1 Trim any fat from the beef and cut into about 24 evenly sized pieces.

2 Thread the meat on to 8 skewers, alternating the pieces with cherry tomatoes and olives.

3 To make the baste, combine the oil, vinegar, garlic and salt and pepper to taste in a bowl.

4 To make the fresh tomato relish, heat the oil in a small pan and fry the onion and garlic for 3–4 minutes until softened. Add the tomatoes and olives and cook for 2–3 minutes until the tomatoes are softened slightly. Stir in the parsley and lemon juice and season with salt and pepper to taste. Set aside and keep warm or leave to chill.

5 Barbecue the skewers on an oiled rack over hot coals for 5–10 minutes, basting and turning frequently. Serve with the tomato relish and slices of focaccia.

Meatball Brochettes

Children will love these tasty meatballs on a skewer, which are economical and easy to make on the barbecue.

NUTRITIONAL INFORMATION

Calories	120	Sugars	........2g
Protein	........17g	Fat	..........5g
Carbohydrate	....2g	Saturates	......2g

10 mins, plus 50 mins soaking/chilling

10 mins

MAKES 8

INGREDIENTS

25 g/1 oz bulgar wheat

350 g/12 oz lean minced beef

1 onion, chopped very finely (optional)

1 tbsp tomato ketchup

1 tbsp brown fruity sauce

1 tbsp chopped fresh parsley

beaten egg, to bind

8 cherry tomatoes

8 button mushrooms

oil, to baste

8 bread finger rolls, to serve

1 Place the bulgar wheat in a bowl and cover with boiling water. Leave to soak for 20 minutes or until softened. Drain thoroughly and leave to cool.

2 Place the soaked wheat, minced beef, onion (if using), ketchup, brown fruity sauce and chopped fresh parsley together in a mixing bowl and mix until all the ingredients are well combined. Add a little beaten egg if necessary to bind the mixture together.

3 Using your hands, shape the meat mixture into 24 evenly-sized balls. Put the meatballs in the refrigerator to chill for 30 minutes.

4 Thread the chilled meatballs on to 8 pre-soaked wooden skewers, alternating them with the cherry tomatoes and button mushrooms.

5 Brush the brochettes with a little oil and barbecue over hot coals for about 10 minutes, until cooked through, turning occasionally and brushing with a little more oil if the meat starts to dry out.

6 Transfer the meatball brochettes to warm serving plates. Cut open the bread finger rolls and push the meat and vegetables off the skewer into the open rolls, using a fork. Serve immediately.

Moroccan Lamb Kebabs

Marinated in Moroccan spices, these barbecued kebabs have a mild spicy flavour. Add the chilli if you like a bit of zip to your meat.

NUTRITIONAL INFORMATION

Calories . . . . . . .348 Sugars 2g
Protein . . . . .30g Fat 24g
Carbohydrate . . . .2g Saturates 10g

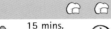

15 mins, plus 2 hrs marinating   10 mins

SERVES 4

INGREDIENTS

450 g/1 lb lean lamb

1 lemon

1 red onion

4 small courgettes

couscous, to serve (see Cook's Tip)

MARINADE

grated rind and juice of 1 lemon

2 tbsp olive oil

1 clove garlic, crushed

1 red chilli, sliced (optional)

1 tsp ground cinnamon

1 tsp ground ginger

½ tsp ground cumin

½ tsp ground coriander

1 Cut the lamb into even, bite-sized chunks, and place in a large, non-metallic dish.

2 To make the marinade, combine the lemon rind and juice, oil, garlic, chilli (if using), ground cinnamon, ginger, cumin and coriander in a bowl.

3 Pour the marinade over the lamb and toss to coat. Cover and leave to marinate in the refrigerator for at least 2 hours, or preferably overnight.

4 Cut the lemon into 8 pieces. Cut the onion into wedges, then separate each wedge into 2 pieces.

5 Using a canelle knife or potato peeler, cut thin strips of peel from the courgettes, then cut the courgettes into even-sized chunks.

6 Remove the meat from the marinade, reserving the liquid for basting. Thread the meat on to skewers alternating with the onion, lemon and courgette.

7 Barbecue over hot coals for 8–10 minutes, turning and basting with the reserved marinade. Serve on a bed of couscous (see Cook's Tip, below).

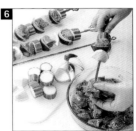

COOK'S TIP

Serve these kebabs with couscous. Allowing 55 g/2 oz couscous per person, soak the couscous in cold water for about 20 minutes until softened. Drain and steam for 10 minutes or until piping hot.

Indian Kofta

Lean minced lamb is mixed with curry paste to produce a flavourful Indian-style kebab, which is served with a refreshing tomato sambal.

NUTRITIONAL INFORMATION

Calories	126	Sugars	.........2g
Protein	........12g	Fat	...........7g
Carbohydrate	....3g	Saturates	.......2g

5 mins, plus 1 hr chilling/standing

10–15 mins

MAKES 8

I N G R E D I E N T S

1 small onion

450 g/1 lb ground lamb

2 tbsp curry paste

2 tbsp natural yogurt

oil, to baste

sprigs of fresh coriander, to garnish

T O M A T O   S A M B A L

3 tomatoes, deseeded and diced

pinch of ground coriander

pinch of ground cumin

2 tsp chopped fresh coriander

salt and pepper

T O   S E R V E

poppadoms

chutney

1 Put the onion in a food processor and chop finely. Add the lamb and process briefly to chop the mince further. This will help the meat mixture to hold together during cooking. If you do not have a food processor, grate the onion finely before mixing it with the lamb.

2 Add the curry paste and yogurt and mix well. Divide the mixture into 8 equal portions.

3 Shape the mixture into 8 sausages and push each one on to a skewer, pressing the mixture together firmly. Chill in the refrigerator for at least 30 minutes.

4 To make the tomato sambal, mix together the tomatoes, spices, chopped coriander and salt and pepper to taste in a bowl. Leave to stand for at least 30 minutes for the flavours to combine.

5 Barbecue the kebabs on an oiled rack over hot coals for 10–15 minutes, turning frequently. Baste with a little oil if required.

6 Transfer to serving plates and garnish with fresh coriander. Serve accompanied with poppadoms, chutney and the tomato sambal.

Pork & Sage Kebabs

Pork mince mixture is shaped into meatballs and threaded on to skewers. They have a delicious, slightly sweet flavour that is popular with children.

NUTRITIONAL INFORMATION

Calories . . . . .96 Sugars 0.1g
Protein . . . . .8g Fat 7g
Carbohydrate . . . .2g Saturates 2g

 5 mins, plus 30 mins chilling 8–10 mins

MAKES 12

I N G R E D I E N T S

450 g/1 lb pork mince

2 tbsp fresh breadcrumbs

1 small onion, very finely chopped

1 tbsp chopped fresh sage

2 tbsp apple sauce

¼ tsp ground nutmeg

salt and pepper

B A S T E

3 tbsp olive oil

1 tbsp lemon juice

T O   S E R V E

6 small pitta breads

mixed salad leaves

6 tbsp thick natural yogurt

1 Place the mince in a mixing bowl together with the breadcrumbs, onion, sage, apple sauce, nutmeg and salt and pepper to taste. Mix until the ingredients are well combined.

VARIATION

Save time by shaping the meat mixture into burgers. Leave to chill for at least 20 minutes, then barbecue, basting with the oil and lemon mixture for 15 minutes, turning once. Serve in burger buns, topped with a little apple sauce.

2 Using your hands, shape the mixture into small balls, about the size of large marbles, and leave to chill in the refrigerator for at least 30 minutes.

3 Meanwhile, soak 12 small wooden skewers in cold water for 30 minutes. Thread the meatballs on to the skewers.

4 To make the baste, mix the oil and lemon juice in a small bowl, whisking with a fork until it is well blended.

5 Barbecue the kebabs over hot coals for 8–10 minutes, turning and basting until the meat is cooked through.

6 Line the pitta breads with the salad leaves and spoon over some of the yogurt. Serve with the kebabs.

Vegetarian Sausages

Deliciously cheesy sausages will be a hit with vegetarians who have no need to feel left out when it comes to tasty barbecued food.

NUTRITIONAL INFORMATION

Calories 213   Sugars 4g
Protein . . . . .8g   Fat 12g
Carbohydrate . . .19g   Saturates 4g

10 mins, plus 30 mins chilling

15–20 mins

MAKES 8

INGREDIENTS

1 tbsp sunflower oil

1 small onion, chopped finely

50 g/1¾ oz mushrooms, finely chopped

½ red pepper, deseeded and chopped finely

400 g/14 oz canned cannellini beans, rinsed and drained

100 g/3½ oz fresh breadcrumbs

100 g/3½ oz Cheddar cheese, grated

1 tsp dried mixed herbs

1 egg yolk

seasoned plain flour, to coat

oil, to baste

TO SERVE

bread rolls

slices of fried onion

1 Heat the oil in a saucepan and fry the prepared onion, mushrooms and peppers until softened.

2 Mash the cannellini beans in a large mixing bowl. Add the onion, mushroom and pepper mixture, and the breadcrumbs, cheese, herbs and egg yolk, and mix together well.

3 Press the mixture together with your fingers and shape into 8 sausages.

4 Roll each sausage in the seasoned flour. Chill for at least 30 minutes.

5 Barbecue the sausages on a sheet of oiled foil set over medium-hot coals for 15–20 minutes, turning and basting frequently with oil, until golden.

6 Split a bread roll down the middle and insert a layer of fried onions. Place the sausage in the roll and serve.

COOK'S TIP

Take care not to break the sausages when turning them over. If you have a hinged rack, oil this and place the sausages inside, turning and oiling frequently. Look out for racks that are especially designed for barbecueing sausages.

Nutty Rice Burgers

Serve these burgers in toasted sesame seed baps. If you wish, add a slice of cheese to top the burger at the end of cooking.

NUTRITIONAL INFORMATION

Calories 517	Sugars 5g
Protein 16g	Fat 26g
Carbohydrate . . .59g	Saturates 6g

5 mins, plus 30 mins chilling

20–25 mins

SERVES 6

INGREDIENTS

1 tbsp sunflower oil

1 small onion, finely chopped

100 g/3½ oz mushrooms, finely chopped

350 g/12 oz cooked brown rice

100 g/3½ oz fresh breadcrumbs

75 g/2¾ oz chopped walnuts

1 egg

2 tbsp brown fruity sauce

dash of Tabasco sauce

salt and pepper

oil, to baste

6 individual cheese slices (optional)

TO SERVE

6 sesame seed baps

slices of onion

slices of tomato

1 Heat the oil in a large saucepan and fry the onions for 3–4 minutes, until they just begin to soften. Add the mushrooms and cook for a further 2 minutes.

2 Remove the pan from the heat and mix the cooked rice, breadcrumbs, walnuts, egg and both the sauces into the vegetables. Season to taste with salt and pepper and mix well again.

3 Shape the mixture into 6 burgers, pressing the mixture together with your fingers. Set aside to chill in the refrigerator for at least 30 minutes.

4 Barbecue the burgers on an oiled rack over medium-hot coals for 5–6 minutes on each side, turning once and frequently basting with oil.

5 If liked, top the burgers with a slice of cheese 2 minutes before the end of the cooking time. Barbecue the onion and tomato slices for 3–4 minutes until they are just beginning to colour.

6 Toast the sesame seed baps at the side of the barbecue. Serve the burgers in the baps, together with the barbecued onions and tomatoes.

COOK'S TIP

It is quicker and more economical to use leftover rice to make these burgers. However, if you are cooking the rice for this dish you will need to use 175 g/6 oz uncooked rice.

Lemon Chicken Skewers

An unusual recipe in which fresh lemon grass stalks are used as skewers, imparting their delicate lemon flavour to the chicken mixture.

NUTRITIONAL INFORMATION

Calories	140	Sugars	.........2g
Protein	........19g	Fat	...........7g
Carbohydrate	....2g	Saturates	.......1g

5 mins, plus 15 mins chilling

4–6 mins

MAKES 8

INGREDIENTS

2 long or 4 short lemon grass stalks

2 large chicken breasts, about 400 g/14 oz in total, skinned and boned

1 small egg white

1 carrot, finely grated

1 small red chilli, deseeded and chopped

2 tbsp chopped fresh garlic chives

2 tbsp chopped fresh coriander

1 tbsp sunflower oil

salt and pepper

fresh coriander and lime slices, to garnish

1 If the lemon grass stalks are long, cut them in half across the middle to make 4 short lengths. Cut each stalk in half lengthways, so you have 8 sticks.

2 Roughly chop the chicken pieces and place them in a food processor with the egg white. Process to a smooth paste, then add the carrot, chilli, chives, coriander and salt and pepper. Process for a few seconds to mix well.

3 Chill the mixture in the refrigerator for about 15 minutes. Divide the mixture into 8 equal portions, and use your hands to shape the mixture firmly around the lemon grass 'skewers'.

4 Brush the skewers with oil and barbecue over hot coals, or grill under a preheated medium-hot grill, for 4–6 minutes, turning them occasionally, until golden brown and thoroughly cooked.

5 Serve while hot, and garnish with sprigs of fresh coriander and slices of lime.

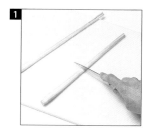

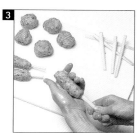

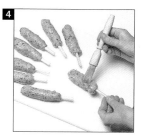

Thai-style Burgers

If your family likes to eat burgers, try these – they have a much more interesting flavour than conventional hamburgers.

NUTRITIONAL INFORMATION

Calories 358	Sugars 1g
Protein 23g	Fat 29g
Carbohydrate 2g	Saturates 5g

 5–10 mins   12–16 mins

SERVES 4

INGREDIENTS

1 small lemon grass stalk

1 small red chilli, deseeded

2 garlic cloves, peeled

2 spring onions

200 g/7 oz closed-cup mushrooms

400 g/14 oz minced pork

1 tbsp Thai fish sauce

3 tbsp chopped fresh coriander

sunflower oil for shallow frying

2 tbsp mayonnaise

1 tbsp lime juice

salt and pepper

TO SERVE

4 sesame hamburger buns

shredded Chinese leaves

1 Place the lemon grass, chilli, garlic and spring onions in a food processor and process to a smooth paste, then add the mushrooms and process until very finely chopped.

2 In a bowl, mix the mushroom paste with the minced pork, fish sauce and coriander. Season well with salt and pepper, then divide the mixture into 4 equal portions and shape with lightly floured hands into flat burger shapes.

3 Cook the burgers over medium-hot coals, or in a frying pan over a medium heat, for 6–8 minutes.

4 Meanwhile, mix the mayonnaise with the lime juice. Split the hamburger buns and spread the lime-flavoured mayonnaise on the cut surfaces. Add a few shredded Chinese leaves, top with a burger and sandwich together. Serve immediately, while still hot.

Chilli-glazed Prawn Skewers

Whole tiger prawns cook very quickly on a barbecue or under a grill so they're ideal for summertime cooking, indoors or outside.

NUTRITIONAL INFORMATION

Calories 106   Sugars 8g
Protein . . . . .11g   Fat 3g
Carbohydrate . . . .8g   Saturates 1g

10 mins, plus 2 hrs chilling   5–6 mins

SERVES 4

INGREDIENTS

1 garlic clove, chopped

1 red bird-eye chilli, deseeded and chopped

1 tbsp tamarind paste

1 tbsp sesame oil

1 tbsp dark soy sauce

2 tbsp lime juice

1 tbsp soft light brown sugar

16 large whole raw tiger prawns

TO SERVE

crusty bread

lime wedges

salad leaves

1 Put the garlic, chilli, tamarind, sesame oil, soy sauce, lime juice and sugar in a small pan. Stir over a low heat until the sugar is dissolved, then remove from the heat and allow to cool completely.

2 Wash and dry the prawns and place in a single layer in a wide, non-metallic dish. Spoon the marinade over the prawns and turn them over to coat evenly. Cover the dish and leave in the refrigerator to marinate for at least 2 hours, or preferably overnight.

3 Meanwhile, soak 4 bamboo or wooden skewers in water for about 20 minutes. Drain and thread 4 prawns on to each skewer.

4 Barbecue the skewers over hot coals, or grill under a preheated hot grill, for 5–6 minutes, turning them over once, until they turn pink and begin to brown.

5 Thread a wedge of fresh lime on to the end of each prawn skewer and serve with crusty bread and salad leaves.

Turkey with Redcurrant Jelly

Prepare these steaks the day before they are needed and serve in toasted ciabatta bread, accompanied by crisp salad leaves.

NUTRITIONAL INFORMATION

Calories 219   Sugars 4g
Protein . . . . .28g   Fat 10g
Carbohydrate . . . .4g   Saturates 1g

 5 mins, plus 12 hrs marinating   8–10 mins

SERVES 4

I N G R E D I E N T S

100 g/3½ oz redcurrant jelly

2 tbsp lime juice

3 tbsp olive oil

2 tbsp dry white wine

¼ tsp ground ginger

pinch grated nutmeg

4 turkey breast steaks

salt and pepper

T O   S E R V E

mixed salad leaves

vinaigrette dressing

1 ciabatta loaf

cherry tomatoes

1 Place the redcurrant jelly and lime juice in a saucepan and heat gently until the jelly melts. Add the oil, wine, ginger and nutmeg.

COOK'S TIP

Turkey and chicken escalopes are also ideal for cooking on the barbecue. Because they are thin, they cook through without burning on the outside. Marinade overnight, and baste with a little lemon juice and oil while cooking.

2 Place the turkey steaks in a shallow, non-metallic dish and season with salt and pepper. Pour over the marinade, turning the meat so that it is well coated. Cover and refrigerate overnight.

3 Remove the turkey from the marinade, reserving the marinade, and barbecue on an oiled rack for about 4 minutes on each side. Baste frequently with the reserved marinade.

4 Meanwhile, toss the salad leaves in the vinaigrette dressing. Cut the ciabatta loaf in half lengthways and place, cut-side down, at the side of the barbecue, until golden. Place each steak on top of a salad leaf, sandwich between 2 pieces of bread and serve with cherry tomatoes.

Tofu Skewers

Altough tofu is rather bland on its own, it develops a fabulous flavour when it is marinated in garlic and herbs.

NUTRITIONAL INFORMATION

Calories	149	Sugars	.........5g
Protein	........13g	Fat	...........9g
Carbohydrate	....5g	Saturates	......1g

15 mins, plus 20–30 mins marinating   6 mins

SERVES 4

INGREDIENTS

350 g/12 oz tofu

1 red pepper

1 yellow pepper

2 courgettes

8 button mushrooms

slices of lemon, to garnish

MARINADE

grated rind and juice of ½ lemon

1 clove garlic, crushed

½ tsp chopped fresh rosemary

½ tsp chopped fresh thyme

1 tbsp walnut oil

1 To make the marinade, combine the lemon rind and juice, garlic, rosemary, thyme and oil in a shallow dish.

2 Drain the tofu, pat it dry with kitchen paper and cut it into squares. Add to the marinade and toss to coat. Leave to marinate for 20–30 minutes.

3 Meanwhile, deseed and cut the peppers into 2.5 cm/1 inch pieces. Blanch in boiling water for 4 minutes, refresh in cold water and drain.

4 Using a canelle knife or potato peeler, remove strips of peel from the courgettes. Cut the courgette into 2.5 cm/1 inch chunks.

5 Remove the tofu from the marinade, reserving the liquid for basting. Thread the tofu on to 8 skewers, alternating with the peppers, courgette and button mushrooms.

6 Barbecue the skewers over medium hot coals for about 6 minutes, turning and basting with the marinade. Transfer the skewers to warm serving plates, garnish with slices of lemon and serve.

Garlic Potato Wedges

Serve this tasty potato dish with barbecued kebabs, bean burgers or vegetarian sausages.

NUTRITIONAL INFORMATION

Calories 257	Sugars 1g
Protein 3g	Fat 16g
Carbohydrate ...26g	Saturates 5g

 10 mins   30–35 mins

SERVES 4

I N G R E D I E N T S

3 large baking potatoes, scrubbed

4 tbsp olive oil

2 tbsp butter

2 garlic cloves, chopped

1 tbsp chopped fresh rosemary

1 tbsp chopped fresh parsley

1 tbsp chopped fresh thyme

salt and pepper

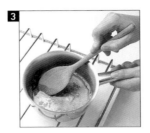

1 Bring a large pan of water to the boil, add the potatoes and parboil them for 10 minutes. Drain the potatoes, refresh under cold water and then drain them again thoroughly.

2 Transfer the potatoes to a chopping board. When cold enough to handle, cut into thick wedges, but do not peel.

3 Heat the oil, butter and garlic in a small pan. Cook gently until the garlic begins to brown, then remove the pan from the heat.

4 Stir the herbs and salt and pepper to taste into the mixture in the pan.

5 Brush the warm garlic and herb mixture generously over the parboiled potato wedges.

6 Barbecue the potatoes over hot coals for 10–15 minutes, brushing liberally with any of the remaining garlic and herb mixture, or until the potato wedges are just tender.

7 Transfer the garlic potato wedges to a warm serving plate and serve as a starter or side dish.

COOK'S TIP

You may find it easier to barbecue or grill these potatoes in a hinged rack or in a specially designed barbecue or grill roasting tray.

Stuffed Tomatoes

These barbecued tomato cups are filled with a delicious Greek-style combination of herbs, nuts and raisins.

NUTRITIONAL INFORMATION

Calories ....156 Sugars 10g
Protein ....3g Fat 7g
Carbohydrate ...22g Saturates 0.7g

10 mins   10 mins

SERVES 4

INGREDIENTS

4 beef tomatoes

300 g/10½ oz cooked rice

8 spring onions, chopped

3 tbsp chopped fresh mint

2 tbsp chopped fresh parsley

3 tbsp pine kernels

3 tbsp raisins

2 tsp olive oil

salt and pepper

1 Cut the tomatoes in half, then scoop out the seeds and discard.

2 Stand the tomatoes upside down on absorbent kitchen paper for a few moments to allow the juices to drain out, then turn the shells the right way up and sprinkle the insides with salt and pepper.

3 Mix together the rice, spring onions, mint, parsley, pine kernels and raisins.

4 Spoon the rice mixture into the tomato cups.

5 Drizzle a little olive oil over the stuffed tomatoes, then barbecue on an oiled rack over medium-hot coals for about 10 minutes until they are tender and cooked through.

6 Transfer the barbecued tomatoes to serving plates and serve immediately, while still hot.

COOK'S TIP

Tomatoes are a popular barbecue vegetable. Try grilling slices of beef tomato and slices of onion, brushed with a little oil and topped with sprigs of fresh herbs; or thread cherry tomatoes on to skewers and barbecue for 5–10 minutes.

Colourful Kebabs

Brighten up a barbecue meal with these colourful vegetable kebabs. They are basted with an aromatic, flavoured oil.

NUTRITIONAL INFORMATION

Calories 131   Sugars 7g
Protein . . . . .2g   Fat 11g
Carbohydrate . . . .8g   Saturates 2g

15 mins   15 mins

SERVES 4

INGREDIENTS

1 red pepper, deseeded

1 yellow pepper, deseeded

1 green pepper, deseeded

1 small onion

8 cherry tomatoes

100 g/3½ oz wild mushrooms

SEASONED OIL

6 tbsp olive oil

1 garlic clove, crushed

½ tsp mixed dried herbs or herbes de Provence

1 Cut the deseeded peppers into 2.5 cm/1 inch pieces.

2 Peel the onion and cut it into wedges, leaving the root end just intact to help keep the wedges together.

3 Thread the pepper pieces, onion wedges, tomatoes and mushrooms on to skewers, alternating the colours of the peppers.

4 To make the seasoned oil, mix together the olive oil, garlic and mixed herbs or herbes de Provence in a small bowl. Brush the mixture liberally over the kebabs.

5 Barbecue the kebabs over medium hot coals for 10–15 minutes, brushing with the seasoned oil and turning the skewers frequently.

6 Transfer the vegetable kebabs on to warmed serving plates. Serve the kebabs immediately, accompanied by a rich walnut sauce (see Cook's Tip, below), if you wish.

COOK'S TIP

To make walnut sauce, process 125 g/4½ oz walnuts in a food processor to a smooth paste. With the machine running, add 150 ml/5 fl oz double cream and 1 tablespoon of olive oil. Season to taste with salt and pepper.

Buttery Corn-on-the-cob

There are a number of ways of cooking corn-on-the-cob on a barbecue. Leaving on the husks protects the tender corn niblets.

NUTRITIONAL INFORMATION

Calories 79   Sugars 2g
Protein . . . . .3g   Fat 2g
Carbohydrate . . .14g   Saturates 0.2g

  10 mins   20–30 mins

SERVES 4

I N G R E D I E N T S

4 sweetcorn cobs, with husks

100 g/3½ oz butter

1 tbsp chopped fresh parsley

1 tsp chopped fresh chives

1 tsp chopped fresh thyme

grated rind of 1 lemon

salt and pepper

1 To prepare the cobs of sweetcorn, peel back the husks to the base and remove the silken hairs.

2 Fold back the husks and secure them in place with string if necessary.

3 Blanch the cobs in a large saucepan of boiling water for about 5 minutes. Remove with a perforated spoon and drain thoroughly.

4 Barbecue the cobs over medium hot coals for 20–30 minutes, turning frequently to cook evenly.

5 Meanwhile, soften the butter and beat in the parsley, chives, thyme, lemon rind and salt and pepper to taste.

6 Transfer the cobs to serving plates, remove the string and pull back the husks. Serve with the herb butter.

COOK'S TIP

If you are unable to get fresh cobs, frozen cobs can be cooked on the barbecue. Spread some of the herb butter on to a sheet of double thickness foil. Wrap the cobs in the foil and barbecue among the coals for 20–30 minutes.

Coleslaw

Home-made coleslaw tastes far superior to any that you can buy. If you make it in advance, add the sunflower seeds just before serving.

NUTRITIONAL INFORMATION

Calories 224	Sugars 8g
Protein 3g	Fat 20g
Carbohydrate 8g	Saturates 3g

 10 mins   5 mins

SERVES 4

INGREDIENTS

150 ml/5 fl oz low-fat mayonnaise

150 ml/5 fl oz low-fat natural yogurt

dash of Tabasco sauce

1 medium head of white cabbage

4 carrots

1 green pepper

2 tbsp sunflower seeds

salt and pepper

1 To make the dressing, combine the mayonnaise, yogurt, Tabasco sauce and salt and pepper to taste in a small bowl. Leave to chill until required.

2 Cut the cabbage in half and then into quarters. Remove and discard the tough centre stalk. Shred the cabbage leaves finely. Wash the leaves and dry them thoroughly.

VARIATION

To give the coleslaw a slightly different flavour and texture, try adding one or more of the following ingredients: raisins, grapes, grated apple, chopped walnuts, cubes of cheese or roasted peanuts.

3 Peel the carrots and shred using a food processor or a mandolin. Alternatively, coarsely grate the carrot.

4 Quarter and deseed the pepper and cut the flesh into thin strips.

5 Combine the vegetables in a large bowl and toss to mix. Pour over the dressing and toss until the vegetables are coated. Chill until required.

6 Just before serving, place the sunflower seeds on a baking tray and toast them in the oven or under the grill until golden brown. Transfer the salad to a large serving dish, scatter with sunflower seeds and serve.

Spinach & Orange Salad

This is a refreshing and very nutritious salad. Add the dressing just before serving so that the leaves do not become soggy.

NUTRITIONAL INFORMATION

Calories 126   Sugars 10g
Protein ....3g   Fat 9g
Carbohydrate ...10g   Saturates 1g

10 mins   0 mins

SERVES 4

INGREDIENTS

225 g/8 oz baby spinach leaves

2 large oranges

½ red onion

DRESSING

3 tbsp extra virgin olive oil

2 tbsp freshly squeezed orange juice

2 tsp lemon juice

1 tsp clear honey

½ tsp wholegrain mustard

salt and pepper

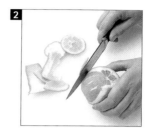

1 Wash the spinach leaves under cold running water, then dry them thoroughly on absorbent kitchen paper. Remove any tough stalks and tear the larger leaves into smaller pieces.

2 Slice the top and bottom off each orange with a sharp knife, then remove the peel. Carefully slice between the membranes of the orange to remove the segments. Reserve any juices for the salad dressing.

3 Using a sharp knife, finely chop the red onion.

4 Mix together the spinach leaves and orange segments and arrange in a serving dish or in individual dishes.

5 Scatter the chopped onion over the top of the salad.

6 To make the dressing, whisk together the olive oil, orange juice, lemon juice, honey, mustard and salt and pepper to taste in a small bowl.

7 Pour the dressing over the salad just before serving. Toss the salad well to coat the leaves with the dressing.

Mozzarella & Tomato Salad

Take advantage of the delicious varieties of cherry tomatoes that are available to make a refreshing Italian-style salad with lots of eye-appeal.

NUTRITIONAL INFORMATION

Calories 295	Sugars 3g	
Protein 9g	Fat 27g	
Carbohydrate 3g	Saturates 7g	

5 mins, plus 4 hrs chilling   0 mins

SERVES 4

INGREDIENTS

450 g/1 lb cherry tomatoes

4 spring onions

125 ml/4 fl oz extra virgin olive oil

2 tbsp best-quality balsamic vinegar

200 g/7 oz buffalo mozzarella (see Cook's Tip), cut into cubes

15 g/½ oz fresh flat leaf parsley

25 g/1 oz fresh basil leaves

salt and pepper

1 Using a sharp knife, cut the tomatoes in half and put in a large bowl. Trim the spring onions, finely chop the green and white parts, then add to the bowl.

2 Pour in the olive oil and balsamic vinegar and use your hands to toss together. Season with salt and pepper, add the mozzarella and toss again. Cover and chill for 4 hours.

3 Remove from the refrigerator 10 minutes before serving. Finely chop the parsley and add to the salad. Tear the basil leaves over the salad and toss all the ingredients together again. Adjust the seasoning and serve.

COOK'S TIP

For the best flavour, buy buffalo mozzarella – *mozzarella di bufala* – rather than the factory-made cow's milk version. This salad would also look good made with bocconcini which are small balls of mozzarella. Look out for these in Italian delicatessens.

Panzanella

This traditional, refreshing Italian salad of day-old bread is ideal as a simple supper on a hot day. It is packed with Mediterranean flavours.

NUTRITIONAL INFORMATION

Calories 213   Sugars 11g
Protein . . . . .7g   Fat 6g
Carbohydrate . . .33g   Saturates 1g

10–15 mins, plus 30 mins standing

0 mins

SERVES 4-6

I N G R E D I E N T S

250 g/9 oz stale focaccia, ciabatta or French bread

4 large, vine-ripened tomatoes

extra virgin olive oil

4 red, yellow and/or orange peppers

100 g/3½ oz cucumber

1 large red onion, finely chopped

8 canned anchovy fillets, drained and chopped

2 tbsp capers in brine, rinsed and patted dry

about 4 tbsp red wine vinegar

about 2 tbsp best-quality balsamic vinegar

salt and pepper

fresh basil leaves, to garnish

1 Cut the bread into 2.5 cm/1 inch cubes and place in a large serving bowl. Working over a plate to catch any juices, quarter the tomatoes. Reserve the juices. Using a teaspoon, scoop out the cores and seeds and discard, then finely chop the flesh. Add the chopped flesh to the bread cubes.

2 Drizzle 5 tablespoons of olive oil over the mixture and toss with your hands until well coated. Pour in the reserved tomato juice and toss again. Set aside for about 30 minutes.

3 Meanwhile, cut the peppers in half, remove the cores and seeds. Place under a preheated hot grill for 10 minutes, until the skins are charred and the flesh is tender. Place in a plastic bag, seal and set aside for 20 minutes to allow the steam to loosen the skins, then remove the skins and finely chop.

4 Cut the cucumber in half lengthways, then cut each half into 3 strips, lengthways. Using a teaspoon, scoop out and discard the seeds. Dice the cucumber.

5 Add the onion, peppers, cucumber, anchovy fillets and capers to the bread and toss. Sprinkle with the red wine and balsamic vinegars and season to taste. Drizzle with extra olive oil or vinegar if necessary, but make sure it does not become too greasy or soggy. Sprinkle the fresh basil leaves over the salad and serve.

Green Tabbouleh

Tomatoes are sometimes included in this refreshing bulgar wheat salad from Turkey, but this version relies on herbs and vegetables for its flavour.

NUTRITIONAL INFORMATION

Calories ....333 Sugars 2g
Protein ....9g Fat 7g
Carbohydrate ...59g Saturates 1g

10 mins, plus 20 mins soaking

0 mins

SERVES 4-6

INGREDIENTS

300 g/10½ oz bulgar wheat

200 g/7 oz cucumber

6 spring onions

15 g/½ oz fresh flat leaf parsley

1 unwaxed lemon

about 2 tbsp garlic-flavoured olive oil

salt and pepper

1 Bring a kettle of water to the boil. Place the bulgar wheat in a heatproof bowl, pour over 600 ml/1 pint of the boiling water and cover with an upturned plate. Set aside for at least 20 minutes until the wheat absorbs the water and becomes tender.

2 While the wheat is soaking, cut the cucumber in half lengthways and then cut each half into 3 strips lengthways. Using a teaspoon, scoop out and discard the seeds. Chop the cucumber strips into bite-sized pieces and place in a serving bowl.

3 Trim the top of the green parts of each of the spring onions, then cut each in half lengthways. Finely chop and add to the cucumber.

4 Place the fresh parsley on a chopping board and sprinkle with salt. Using a cook's knife, very finely chop both the leaves and the stems. Add to the bowl with the chopped cucumber and onions. Finely grate the rind from the unwaxed lemon into the bowl.

5 When the bulgar wheat is cool enough to handle, either squeeze out any excess water with your hands or press out the water through a sieve, then add to the bowl with the other ingredients.

6 Cut the lemon in half and squeeze the juice of one half over the salad. Add 2 tablespoons of the garlic-flavoured oil and stir all the ingredients together. Adjust the seasoning with salt and pepper to taste, and add extra lemon juice or oil if needed. Cover and chill until required.

Spiced Pilau with Saffron

A Middle Eastern influence is evident in this fragrant pilau, studded with nuts, fruit and spices. This rice is ideal served with barbecued lamb.

NUTRITIONAL INFORMATION

Calories	347	Sugars	.........9g
Protein	.........5g	Fat	...........11g
Carbohydrate	...60g	Saturates	.......3g

2 mins, plus 35 mins infusing/standing

25 mins

SERVES 4–6

INGREDIENTS

large pinch of good-quality saffron threads

450 ml/16 fl oz boiling water

1 tsp salt

2 tbsp butter

2 tbsp olive oil

1 large onion, very finely chopped

3 tbsp pine kernels

350 g/12 oz long-grain rice (not basmati)

55 g/2 oz sultanas or raisins

6 green cardamom pods, shells lightly cracked

6 cloves

pepper

very finely chopped fresh coriander or flat leaf parsley, to garnish

1 Toast the saffron threads in a dry frying pan over a medium heat, stirring, for 2 minutes, until they give off an aroma. Immediately tip on to a plate.

2 Pour the boiling water into a measuring jug, stir in the saffron and salt and set aside for 30 minutes to infuse.

3 Melt the butter and oil in a frying pan over a medium-high heat. Add the onion. Cook for about 5 minutes, stirring.

4 Lower the heat, stir the pine kernels into the onions and continue cooking for 2 minutes, stirring, until the kernels just start to turn golden. Take care not to let them burn.

5 Stir in the rice, coating all the grains with oil. Stir for 1 minute, then add the sultanas, cardamom pods and cloves. Pour in the saffron-flavoured water and bring to the boil. Lower the heat, then cover and simmer for 15 minutes without removing the lid.

6 Remove from the heat and stand for 5 minutes without uncovering. Remove the lid and check that the rice is tender, the liquid has been absorbed and the surface has small indentations all over.

7 Fluff up the rice and adjust the seasoning. Stir in the herbs and serve.

Lemon & Basil Rice

Jasmine rice has a delicate flavour and can be served completely plain. This simple recipe adds the light tang of lemon and soft scent of basil.

NUTRITIONAL INFORMATION

Calories	384	Sugars	.........0g
Protein	.........7g	Fat	...........4g
Carbohydrate	...86g	Saturates	.......1g

5 mins, plus 10 mins standing   15 mins

SERVES 6–8

INGREDIENTS

400 g/14 oz jasmine rice

800 ml/1⅓ pints water

finely grated rind of ½ lemon

2 tbsp chopped fresh sweet basil

1 Wash the rice in several changes of cold water until the water runs clear. Bring the water to the boil in a large pan, then add the rice.

2 Bring the water back to a rolling boil. Turn the heat to a low simmer, cover the pan and continue simmering for 12 minutes.

3 Remove the pan from the heat and leave to stand, covered, for 10 minutes.

4 Fluff up the rice with a fork, then stir in the lemon rind. Serve scattered with basil.

COOK'S TIP

It is important to leave the pan tightly covered while the rice cooks and steams inside so the grains cook evenly and become fluffy and separate.

Roasted Thai-spiced Peppers

A colourful side dish that also makes a good barbecue party salad. This is best made in advance to give time for the flavours to mingle.

NUTRITIONAL INFORMATION

Calories . . . . .83 Sugars 17g
Protein . . . . .2g Fat 1g
Carbohydrate . . .17g Saturates 0.1g

  5 mins, plus 1½hrs cooling/chilling   10 mins

SERVES 4

INGREDIENTS

2 red peppers

2 yellow peppers

2 green peppers

2 red bird-eye chillies, deseeded and finely chopped

1 lemon grass stalk, finely shredded

4 tbsp lime juice

2 tbsp palm sugar

1 tbsp Thai fish sauce

1 Barbecue the peppers over hot coals, or roast under a hot grill or in a hot oven, turning them over occasionally, until the skins are charred. Cool slightly, then remove the skins. Cut each pepper in half and remove the core and seeds.

2 Slice the skinned peppers thickly and transfer to a large mixing bowl.

3 Place the chillies, lemon grass, lime juice, sugar and fish sauce in a screw-top jar and shake well until thoroughly mixed.

4 Pour the dressing evenly over the peppers while they are still warm. Allow to cool completely, cover with cling film and chill in the refrigerator for at least 1 hour before serving. Transfer to a serving dish to serve.

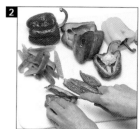

Papaya & Avocado Salad

This colourful and refreshing salad, with its sweet and spicy flavours, is the perfect accompaniment to barbecued food.

NUTRITIONAL INFORMATION

Calories	194	Sugars	.........7g
Protein	.........4g	Fat	..........16g
Carbohydrate	....9g	Saturates	.......3g

 10 mins   0 mins

SERVES 4–6

INGREDIENTS

200 g/7 oz mixed green salad leaves

2–3 spring onions, chopped

3–4 tbsp chopped fresh coriander

1 small papaya

2 red peppers

1 avocado

1 tbsp lime juice

3–4 tbsp pumpkin seeds, preferably toasted (optional)

DRESSING

juice of 1 lime

large pinch of paprika

large pinch of ground cumin

large pinch of sugar

1 garlic clove, finely chopped

4 tbsp extra virgin olive oil

dash of white wine vinegar (optional)

salt

1 Combine the salad leaves with the spring onions and fresh coriander. Mix thoroughly, then transfer the salad to a large serving dish.

2 Cut the papaya in half and scoop out the seeds with a spoon. Cut into quarters, remove the peel and slice the flesh. Arrange on top of the salad leaves.

Cut the peppers in half, remove the cores and seeds, then slice thinly. Add the peppers to the salad leaves.

3 Cut the avocado in half around the stone. Twist apart, then remove the stone with a knife. Carefully peel off the skin, dice the flesh and toss in lime juice to prevent the avocado from discolouring. Add to the other salad ingredients.

4 To make the dressing, whisk together the lime juice, paprika, ground cumin, sugar, chopped garlic and olive oil. Add salt to taste.

5 Pour the dressing over the salad and toss lightly, adding a dash of wine vinegar if a flavour with more 'bite' is preferred. Sprinkle with the toasted pumpkin seeds, if using.

Barbecued Baked Apples

When they are wrapped in foil, apples bake to perfection on the barbecue and make a delightful finale to any meal.

NUTRITIONAL INFORMATION

Calories 294   Sugars 30g
Protein ....3g   Fat 18g
Carbohydrate ...31g   Saturates 7g

5 mins   25–30 mins

SERVES 4

I N G R E D I E N T S

4 medium cooking apples

2 tbsp walnuts, chopped

2 tbsp ground almonds

2 tbsp light muscovado sugar

2 tbsp chopped cherries

2 tbsp chopped stem ginger

1 tbsp almond-flavoured liqueur (optional)

4 tbsp butter

single cream or natural yogurt, to serve

1 Core the apples and using a sharp knife, score each one around the middle to prevent the apple skins from splitting during barbecueing.

2 To make the filling, mix together the walnuts, almonds, sugar, cherries, ginger and almond-flavoured liqueur, if using, in a bowl.

3 Spoon the filling mixture into each apple, pushing it down into the hollowed-out core. Mound a little of the filling mixture on top of each apple.

4 Place each apple on a large square of double thickness foil and generously dot with the butter. Wrap up the foil so that the apple is completely enclosed.

5 Barbecue the foil parcels containing the apples over hot coals for 25–30 minutes or until tender.

6 Transfer the apples to warm, individual serving plates. Serve with lashings of whipped single cream or thick natural yogurt.

COOK'S TIP

If the coals are dying down, place the foil parcels directly on to the coals, raking them up around the apples. Barbecue for 25–30 minutes and serve with the cream or yogurt.

Baked Bananas

The orange-flavoured cream can be prepared in advance, but do not make up the banana parcels until just before you need to cook them.

NUTRITIONAL INFORMATION

Calories ....380 Sugars 40g
Protein ....2g Fat 18g
Carbohydrate ...43g Saturates 11g

 10 mins   10 mins

SERVES 4

INGREDIENTS

4 bananas

2 passion fruit

4 tbsp orange juice

4 tbsp orange-flavoured liqueur

ORANGE-FLAVOURED CREAM

150 ml/5 fl oz double cream

3 tbsp icing sugar

2 tbsp orange-flavoured liqueur

1 To make the orange-flavoured cream, pour the double cream into a mixing bowl and sprinkle over the icing sugar. Whisk the mixture until it is standing in soft peaks. Carefully fold in the orange-flavoured liqueur and chill in the refrigerator until required.

2 Peel the bananas and place each one on to a sheet of kitchen foil.

3 Cut the passion fruit in half and squeeze the juice of each half over each banana. Spoon over the orange juice and liqueur.

4 Fold the kitchen foil over the top of the bananas so that they are completely enclosed.

5 Place the parcels on a baking tray and bake the bananas in a preheated oven, 180°C/350°F/Gas Mark 4, for about 10 minutes, or until they are just tender (test by inserting a cocktail stick).

6 Transfer the foil parcels to warm, individual serving plates. Open out the parcels at the table and serve immediately with the chilled orange-flavoured cream.

VARIATION

Leave the bananas in their skins for a really quick dessert. Split the banana skins and pop in 1–2 cubes of chocolate. Wrap the bananas in kitchen foil and bake for 10 minutes or until the chocolate just melts.

Piña Colada Pineapple

The flavours of pineapple and coconut blend well together, as they do in the well-known drink, Piña Colada.

NUTRITIONAL INFORMATION

Calories 231   Sugars 22g
Protein . . . . .1g   Fat 15g
Carbohydrate . . .22g   Saturates 11g

  10 mins   15–20 mins

SERVES 4

I N G R E D I E N T S

1 small pineapple

4 tbsp unsalted butter

2 tbsp light muscovado sugar

50 g/1¾ oz fresh coconut, grated

2 tbsp coconut-flavoured liqueur or rum

1 Using a very sharp knife, cut the pineapple into quarters and remove the tough core from the centre, leaving the leaves attached.

2 Carefully cut the pineapple flesh away from the skin. Make horizontal cuts across the pineapple quarters.

3 Place the butter in a saucepan and heat gently until melted, stirring continuously. Brush the melted butter over the pineapple and sprinkle with the sugar.

4 Cover the pineapple leaves with kitchen foil to prevent them from burning and transfer them to a rack set over hot coals.

5 Barbecue the pineapple for about 10 minutes.

6 Sprinkle the coconut over the pineapple and barbecue, cut side up, for a further 5–10 minutes, or until the pineapple is piping hot.

7 Transfer the pineapple to serving plates and remove the foil from the leaves. Spoon a little coconut-flavoured liqueur or rum over the pineapple and serve immediately.

COOK'S TIP

Fresh coconut has the best flavour for this dish. If you prefer, however, you can substitute desiccated coconut instead.

Peaches & Mascarpone

If you prepare these in advance, all you have to do is pop the peaches on the barbecue when you are ready to serve them.

NUTRITIONAL INFORMATION

Calories	301	Sugars	.......24g
Protein	.........6g	Fat	.........20g
Carbohydrate	...24g	Saturates	.......9g

 5 mins   5–10 mins

SERVES 4

INGREDIENTS

4 peaches

175 g/6 oz mascarpone cheese

40 g/1½ oz pecan nuts or walnuts, chopped

1 tsp sunflower oil

4 tbsp maple syrup

VARIATION

You can use nectarines instead of peaches for this recipe. Remember to choose ripe but firm fruit which won't go soft and mushy when it is barbecued. Prepare the nectarines in the same way as the peaches and barbecue for 5–10 minutes.

1 Cut the peaches in half and remove the stones. If you are preparing this recipe in advance, press the peach halves together again and wrap them in cling film until required.

2 Mix the mascarpone cheese and chopped pecans or walnuts together in a small bowl, stirring until thoroughly combined. Leave to chill in the refrigerator until required.

3 To serve, brush the peaches with a little oil and place on a rack set over medium-hot coals. Barbecue for 5–10 minutes, turning once, until hot.

4 Transfer the peaches to a serving dish and top with the mascarpone mixture.

5 Drizzle the maple syrup over the peaches and mascarpone filling and serve at once.

Exotic Fruit Parcels

Delicious pieces of exotic fruit are warmed through in a deliciously scented sauce to make a fabulous barbecue dessert.

NUTRITIONAL INFORMATION

Calories 43	Sugars 9g
Protein 2g	Fat 0.3g
Carbohydrate 9g	Saturates 0.1g

10 mins, plus 30 mins marinating

15–20 mins

SERVES 4

I N G R E D I E N T S

1 papaya

1 mango

1 star fruit

1 tbsp grenadine

3 tbsp orange juice

single cream or low-fat natural yogurt, to serve

1 Cut the papaya in half, scoop out the seeds and discard them. Peel the papaya and cut the flesh into thick slices.

2 Prepare the mango by cutting it in half lengthways around the central stone and carefully twisting the fruit off the stone.

3 Score each mango half in a criss-cross pattern. Push each mango half inside out to separate the cubes and cut them away from the peel.

4 Using a sharp knife, thickly slice the star fruit.

5 Place all of the fruit in a bowl and mix them together.

6 Mix the grenadine and orange juice together and pour over the fruit. Leave to marinate for at least 30 minutes.

7 Divide the fruit among 4 double thickness squares of kitchen foil and gather up the edges to form a parcel that encloses the fruit.

8 Place the foil parcel on a rack set over warm coals and barbecue the fruit for 15–20 minutes.

9 Serve the fruit in the parcel, with the low-fat natural yogurt.

COOK'S TIP
Grenadine is a sweet syrup made from pomegranates. If you prefer you could use pomegranate juice instead. To extract the juice, cut the pomegranate in half and squeeze gently with a lemon squeezer – do not press too hard or the juice may become bitter.

This is a Parragon Book
This edition published in 2002

Parragon
Queen Street House
4 Queen Street
Bath BA1 1HE, UK

ISBN: 0-75257-720-4

Printed in China

NOTE

This book uses metric and imperial measurements. Follow the same units of
measurement throughout; do not mix metric and imperial. All spoon measurements
are level: teaspoons are assumed to be 5 ml and tablespoons are assumed to be 15 ml.
Unless otherwise stated, milk is assumed to be full fat, eggs and individual vegetables
such as potatoes are medium and pepper is freshly ground black pepper.

The nutritional information provided for each recipe is per serving or per person.
Optional ingredients, variations or serving suggestions have not been included in the
calculations. The times given for each recipe are an approximate guide only because
the preparation times may differ according to the techniques used by different
people and the cooking times may vary as a result of the type of oven used.

Recipes using raw or very lightly cooked eggs should be
avoided by infants, the elderly, pregnant women, convalescents
and anyone suffering from an illness.